Nights on the Heights

PETER LANG
New York • Bern • Frankfurt am Main • Paris

Giuseppe Bonaviri

Nights on the Heights

translated by
Giovanni R. Bussino

PETER LANG
New York • Bern • Frankfurt am Main • Paris

Library of Congress Cataloging-in-Publication Data

Bonaviri, Giuseppe
  [Notti sull'altura. English]
  Nights on the heights / Giuseppe Bonaviri : Giovanni
Bussino, translator.
    p. cm.
  Translation of: Notti sull'altura.
  "Forms a trilogy with La divina foresta (The divine
forest) (1969) and L'isola amorosa (The loving island)
(1973)"–Pref.
  Includes bibliographical references.
  I. Title.
PQ4862.0496N613 1990   853'.914 – dc20   90-40033
ISBN 0-8204-1355-0   CIP
Cover design by Hank Cutrona.

© Peter Lang Publishing, Inc., New York 1990

Printed in the United States of America.

Nights on the Heights

Preface

Giuseppe Bonaviri's *Notti sull'altura (Nights on the Heights)* (1971), the second of the eleven novels he has written to date, is a fascinating work. It forms a trilogy with *La divina foresta (The Divine Forest)* (1969) and *L'isola amorosa (The Loving Island)* (1973), each dealing with exploratory travel, incredible pursuits or, more precisely, with profound metaphysical quests.

In *Nights on the Heights*, the collective and individual search for an understanding of death (and, by reflection, its counterpart, life) becomes the dominant theme from the very beginning of the novel. Indeed, death, symbolized by the elusive, mysterious "thanatobird," first mentioned in an early chapter, gives the work a powerful unity.

The novel, if indeed it can be called that, is not the fruit of any specific literary current: it is as far from Neorealism as it is from the more recent avant-garde isms. Nor does it have much in common with contemporary semiological fiction, where the only reality is the text itself and where the author's conceits are often buried in a vast verbiage, a wearing thicket of occulist lore and erudition. It is untypical in its range, sensitivity and mode of expression. An experimental work vaguely reminiscent of Proust's *A la recherche* because of its revitalization of past impressions, and of the writings of Buzzati or those of García Márquez because of its magical atmosphere, it investigates new literary directions as yet unattempted by other writers—both Italian and non-Italian.

Should anyone wish to compare this work to any of the late Calvino, another prolific and imaginative modernist, let him first consider the words of Bonaviri himself, who stated in a recent interview: "Both Calvino and I wrote against the prevailing current, and this is the only trait that our works share. Besides, the civilizations that we reflect are completely different, in reality and in fantasy."

Since the work eludes simple characterization, most of the critics, in seeking to describe it, have found it necessary to recur to binomial adjectives, such as, arcane-fantastic, mythic-cosmic, ecologic-magic, anthropo-cosmogonic, lyrico-cosmologic and scientific-philosophic.

This challenging novel of ideas, a distillation of a broad spectrum of the author's scholarship and life experiences, was obviously intended for the mature, learned reader, but it can also be enjoyed by any intelligent person as fantastic narration on a simpler, literal level.

The plot, in part autobiographical, might at first appear traditional: it tells the story of the narrator's return to his birthplace upon the demise of his patriarchal father, and the ensuing exploration of a universe that has that small Sicilian town at its center. But the story line, an account of the persons, places and things encountered during the tangled journey, and, more importantly, of the ideas spawned and discussed all the while, is far from ordinary. It is a delightful fusion of myth and reality, resulting in odd, sometimes dazzling surprises on almost every page.

The events recounted generally unfold chronologically, but the narrative is scarcely linear; it often moves in a sudden zigzag fashion, with numerous anticipations and flashbacks similar to those of a dream. Moreover, there is little character development, each figure being depicted in broad strokes with a minimum of psychological elaboration. As for the denouement, it comes about slowly, as each of the characters in turn meets his or her fate. One would say that Bonaviri, with this work, was bent on completely reconstituting the conventional structure of the novel.

The novel not only entails a physical surveillance of real areas (mainly southeastern Sicily—but also outer space, the center of the earth, and the depths of oceans and seas); it also involves a detailed search into the author's scholarship, a review of his prodigious knowledge of literature (western and oriental), mythology, alchemy, astrology and the various disciplines of ancient and modern science.

Zephir, the author's spokesman, whose name evokes a gentle Sicilian breeze, at first acts as our guide, but as the action disperses in diverse, sometimes simultaneous directions, he virtually becomes a spectator, ceding to a chorus of characters whose queries and comments further the narration.

There have been countless novels that have developed the motif of enlightening travel and adventure. But this unique work extends and widens the scope of that motif, for the expeditions described here, figurative equivalents of existential probings, proceed through multiple dimensions and in every possible direction.

Nature, richly described but not presented as romantic evasion, is a large component of the work, vying with the characters for our attention. Indeed, it functions as a veritable protagonist and, to paraphrase the author, appears as an expansion of his philosophy, or its "physicalization."

As for Bonaviri's diction, except perhaps for some sparse, lively dialogue, it is substantially literary language heightened to an eloquent strangeness by the clever juxtaposition of several choice coinages and learned polysyllables. His prose, which purposely displays an archaic patina, is lyrical, spellbinding, sometimes hypnotic. It incorporates scientific and philosophic concepts of authors who flourished in various periods: from Pre-Socratic writers (e.g., Anaximander, Heraclitus, Empedocles), Classical Roman poets (e.g., Lucretius and Ovid), 17th century thinkers (e.g., Bruno, Majer and Galileo), to modern intellectuals (e.g., Jung, Heidegger and Einstein).

Although the novel as a novel is fictional, autobiographic references abound. The narration, as already intimated, begins with the death of a patriarch, Donnanè (clearly representative of Bonaviri's father, known as Don Nanè [†1964]), and the action takes place primarily in and around Qalat-Minaw, the arabicized equivalent of Mineo, the author's hometown. Moreover, a number of the characters' names (if not their personalities as well) were inspired by Bonaviri's family, relatives and acquaintances. For example,

Emanuele bears the name of the author's fair-haired son; Agrippa derives her name from Agrippina, his aunt; Totosimic is named after the author's uncle Antonio (Totò) and Syssant, mentioned only once, gets his name from one of the author's former Sicilian neighbors, "su-Santo", that is, signor Santo. Ultimately, however, the sketchy autobiographic elements are sublimated to a loftier sphere where myth, magic and metaphor coalesce.

The names of the other characters too were not chosen at random, all being reflective of the author's vast and eclectic knowledge. For instance, Hubble, one of the "scholars," bears the surname of the American astronomer Edwin P. Hubble (1889-1953); Eddington's appellation was suggested by that of the British astronomer Arthur Stanley Eddington (1882-1944); Albumasar gets his name from the medieval Arabic astrologer Abu Mashar; Jafar is named after a famous medieval alchemist, Jafar ibn-Muhammad al-Sadiq; Geber too is named after a well-known medieval alchemist, Abu Musa Jabir ibn-Hayyan; Atman's name can be traced to that of Brahman-Atman of the mystical Hindu text *Upanishads* (c. 900 B.C.); Al-Hakim is the namesake of Al-Hakim, an eleventh-century caliph of the Fatimate dynasty; and, to conclude, Mansur derives his designation from Abu Mansur Muwaffak, a late tenth-century Persian physician. Incidentally, all Arabic words, including proper nouns, are transcribed in the present text according to conventional English usage.

Regarding the time frame of the action, it can best be termed "elastic": the narrator initially travels on an airplane and then in a sports car, and there is mention of laser technology, of the industrial zone of Càtana (Catania) with its chemical pollutants, and of black holes and quasars—all indicating that the adventure takes place in the present century. But such modern allusions coexist with others harkening to a prior historical era, as, for instance, the periodic references to astrolabes and even more primitive means of measuring and calculating celestial phenomena.

The novel, concentrated and thought-provoking, lends itself to several interpretations; indeed, there are various keys that may unlock its significance. For example, it can be read as an indefatigable search for an answer to the ultimate question of human existence as posed by the unbeliever: Is there an afterlife? Indeed, the work appears to be an attempt to free man from the void of biological death in what the author conceives as an animistic or rather hylozoistic universe. It seems an endeavor to assure mankind a place in the cosmos—an effort not only seen in the tireless quests of the characters but also in the three metamorphoses described in the narration, each contemplating the progressive union of man with natural reality. Or, on a more personal level, it seems to figuratively document a valiant intellectual struggle: Bonaviri's effort to find moral consolation in the face of the grim, ineluctable reality of his father's passing. And, since the novel is chock-full of temporal images and concepts, it may similarly be viewed as an allegory of the author's passionate search for the meaning of time (an approach pursued by the critic Franco Zangrilli).

Moreover, the work contains several biblical allusions that touch chords in our memory, evoking a somewhat familiar reality, but the atmosphere, as a whole, appears strangely surrealistic. Suffice it to recall that the names of the characters Yusuf and Aramea suggest those of Joseph and Mary; Diofar could symbolize the infant Jesus; the carob reminds one of the Cross (in medieval art the Cross is often shown as a living tree), and the transplant, a sort of crucifixion; one of the main characters is turned into stone (similar to the fate of Lot's wife); the land of milk and honey traversed by the characters conjures the image of the Promised Land; the father's intellect or mind sought by the characters is reminiscent of the Judeo-Christian idea of the soul that leaves the body at death; the sing-song enumeration of the author's genealogy in Chapter 7 re-echoes a similar procedure employed in *Genesis*, 5; and Nergal's name may have been suggested by a reference in 2 *Kings*, 17, 30.

In brief, this excitingly vital novel, an intellectual treat, will delight readers with the interrelationship and blending of many worlds of experience: ancient and modern philosophy, primitive and contemporary science, religion and superstition. This *contaminatio* or *impasto*, this yoking of diverse realities and contrasting ideas, this fusion of acknowledged dichotomies is a formidable device, resulting in an highly innovative synthesis.

As might have been expected, the language, style and absorbing ideas of the work have not escaped the critics, especially those among the author's compatriots. The most noteworthy (of the thirty or so identified to date) include Italo Calvino, Giuliano Manacorda, Salvatore Battaglia, Enrico Falqui, Walter Pedullà, Ottavio Cecchi, Walter Mauro and, more recently, Gennaro Savarese, Roberto Bertoni, Franco Borrelli and the foregoing Franco Zangrilli.

In conclusion, Bonaviri's *Nights on the Heights*, a microcosm of a literary universe constructed meticulously over several decades (and still expanding), should serve as a splendid introduction to the author's original and sophisticated art. Especially now that Italian fiction is regaining popularity, it is to be hoped that the present translation will encourage further renderings of the author's masterly creations, making them available in the United States, Great Britain, Canada, Australia and wherever there are English-speaking readers who can appreciate fine literature.

G.R.B.

Burbank, California
December, 1989

Introduction

In presenting Bonaviri's first book, *Il sarto della stradalunga* [*The Tailor of Long Street*], in 1954, Elio Vittorini had already observed that the most characteristic element of the author's poetic world was a "delicate cosmic sense." And it is chiefly in developing this motif that Bonaviri succeeded with *La divina foresta* [*The Divine Forest*] (1969) in making the rustic idyll explode into a sort of biological poem. Reading this new book, we are prompted to recall that Vittorini already found in the provincial world of young Bonaviri a reflection of *A Thousand and One Nights*. Now in *Notti sull'altura* [*Nights on the Heights*], the author transfigures the Sicilian landscape of his childhood with arabesque or, if you will, exotic evocations. Mineo, a village in the Ereian Mountains whose poetic space occupies the entire work of the writer, is here called Qalat-Minaw. Although it is modern Sicily that Bonaviri portrays, it is also Sicily as it would have been if the Arabs had remained there, if their culture had not declined and if modern civilization had developed around an astrological, phlogistic, arcane nucleus.

An event, probably autobiographical—the protagonist takes a trip to his birthplace on the occasion of his father's death—is here transfigured into a fantastic pilgrimage. The death of the father is incarnated in a mysterious feathered creature, the "thanatobird," and children, friends, wizards and mystagogues devote themselves to searching for this unreachable bird in the valleys of the eastern portion of Sicily which here take on the names of courses of water from other geographical contexts, as, for example, the Asdrak or the Wadi Hamm.

For Bonaviri, literature—in contrast to medicine, his daily profession—is a return to the past of medical history, toward a natural philosophy dominated by the classification of humors and the properties of stones. The intuition he pursues in this book is that of death "understood as a dimension of biological existence," or, as he writes, "as a simple cerebral dispersal of thousands of psychic perceptions after one's demise." The characters of this novel scatter radially across this Sicilian map composed of all times and all places. In their search for the bird of death, they decipher the signs of minerals and the metamorphoses of plants as if these things constituted a tight network of mysterious relationships.

A mixture of disparate cultural and fantastic materials (occultist, alchemistic, scientific, ethnological) is blended with a repertory of natural images from the memories of a Sicilian childhood. The general design fades into a multicolored delirium, but the movement of the page is always tense, the humor always incisive and the pleasure we get in handling verbal materials and luxurious visual depictions is enough to guarantee the success of this unusual book.

ITALO CALVINO

To my mother

"This infinite which the gods call the supermundane abyss: 'you who know the supermundane paternal abyss.' "

(from the *Orphic Fragments*)

"Learn about eggs and dissect them with a flaming sword. In our world there is a bird which is more sublime than any other; let the search for its egg be your constant preoccupation."

Michail Majer (1568-1622), astrologist.

". . . all the observations and all the data collected with great care do not actually refer to the absolute movements of the planets in space, but to the temporal shifts undergone by the earth-planet conjunction in the course of time."

Alber: Einstein, *Out of My Later Years*

I

After the eighteenth of March, one could no longer resort to the usual empirical observations that when compared to one another yielded general laws suitable for calculating the time of day or for discovering what was happening within us.

For example, I wanted to use the *National Almanac* to determine the node of the lunar orbit, but despite the more than one thousand corrections I repeatedly made for the median longitude our satellite had to occupy up there, almost directly above my head, I was utterly unsuccessful. I was baffled, among other things, by the lack of correspondence between my thoughts and the oscillations coming from those extremely vast spaces shut in by mountains whose massive ridges and clay slopes rose up with an irregular morphology.

Moreover, the sudden news that I had to leave immediately because of what had unexpectedly happened in my hometown threw my fallacious calculations into obvious disorder. So it was useless for me to continue clarifying concepts, seeking semblances of truth or unconditionally accepting contradictory intuitions that sprouted all too readily in my mind. Since I had not done anything unusual during those days, I concluded that everything was running its course in a transformational play of broad or suspended clouds, of hard or round forms and of porous and soft vegetation in the countryside.

I should add that, because of converging circumstances and for the very same reason, young Aramea was with me on the airplane I took at dawn. She was worried about the flight because in her distant region people traveled on foot, and never faster than three miles an hour. Unfortunately, she had had to leave her husband, Yusuf, who could not come since he was busy studying bows, strings and muskets. From time to time she would turn her eyes and loving thoughts to him. She would look eastward with the excuse of peering down from her window at the sea stretched out below us like an immeasurable mirror that the sun's daily rotation multiplied in the luminescent clouds.

When the airplane, leaving those high altitudes, headed toward the mountain peaks and the faded plains of grain, she asked me,

"Oh, are we almost there?"

"As you can see," I replied.

The young woman ran her hand over her black hair, tidying a few locks. We glided down in a short time.

Seeing us coming down the ramp, Atman and my brother, Salvat, greeted us with slow gestures. We immediately left for Qalat-Minaw, where we expected to arrive before noon. Once we were on the road, with my brother at the wheel, we very quickly reached a high speed, dangerously negotiating the few curves, whose edges were covered with wet, green grass. We then passed a succession of eucalyptus trees on both sides of the road, which showered us with rain and revealed a smudged sky above their crowns. Aramea occasionally looked at some horse standing motionless amid the few fields of clover which, farther away, blended with the fleeting images of wide, level clearings.

"It's not like back home," she said.

I felt no attraction to these lands, which appeared blurred and changing because of the speed of the car.

"Everything changes," observed Salvat.

Very soon, in fact, we came upon factories with amorphous domes and pavilions with concrete pavements. Here everything began to look clean and to have glassy curves of impermeable and unbreakable material.

"It's the industrial zone of Càtana," my brother said. I looked drowsily at the algebraically measurable comings and goings of cranes, suspended derricks, trucks and smokestacks emitting granular smoke in continual puffs. The bed of the Simeto was still far away, and its grassy thickets were hidden by bright clouds.

Since we were silent (immersed as we were in curves, segments and noises that reached us from outside), Aramea offered us some dates whose sweetness distracted us somewhat from our thoughts.

"They're good," remarked Salvat, forced to stop because of a small problem with one of the tires. Farther ahead, more than one hundred meters away, a large drill was boring into the ground with strong, rolling movements directed from a command cabin.

Men in overalls were moving through the field in different directions and, resolving a tangle of problems, were conducting systematic research within the layers of earth vomited out in regurgitations.

"Hurry up!" someone shouted.

We set out again, while new rain showers coming straight down darkened the plain, the roofs of the few peasant homes, the first swallows and the tops of the eucalyptuses. Now and again, as the rain increased, long sorties of leaves cascaded from up above.

"To think that before long it'll be spring!" my brother said. Atman nodded as he sat beside the young woman, who was looking at the new branches, the few meadow daisies reclining along the edges of the road and the very low sunlight which was so low that it outlined the dizzy, peculiar movements of a river of changing shapes and blended with strips of barren land, various sorts of grainfields and rows of scarcely visible orange trees. Then Atman said, "The house is probably already full of astronomers and scholars."

"Perhaps," replied Salvat.

We had left the factories behind, and I could still see their shapes in the rearview mirror.

"Oh, the baby!" Aramea suddenly exclaimed, as she gently opened a pocket of her overcoat and pulled out a pouch in which a damp infant wrapped in fringed cotton cloth was screaming (as much as the tight little habitation permitted).

Aramea gave him some milk through a thin straw made of coconut fibers that she introduced into a slit in the pouch. Soon after, little Diofar quieted down and, shutting his tiny eyes, curled up.

"Here's the river," said my brother, as he stepped on the gas to reach the bridge.

The Simeto stretched out along the plain, its low, sandy, grassless banks lazily lapped by slow yellow waters.

"It's half-dry," added Salvat. "The factories are sucking up the river."

I looked toward a terrace beyond the river where an old man with an unlit pipe in his mouth sat on a boulder. Not far away, a great discharge of chemical wastes was flowing into the Simeto in a constant mixture of foaming liquids that reinserted themselves farther ahead into the lifeless, shining river.

"What direction is east?" the young woman asked.

Atman pointed to a stretch of the horizon, while he took notes in a tablet or jotted down countless figures and numbers. But the car's motion bothered him a little. Aramea said, "Everything is brighter over there. Even the clouds are lighter."

She said nothing more because she was thinking about Yusuf, who was working amid long strings, beams and clouds of smoke in a remote place in the east.

The road had now become all curves, but through them we already began to see the orange groves, still full of fruit, that stretched out around us, greeting us with the scent of citrus and saffron.

I still did not know how the event that had made my conjectures even stranger could have occurred so suddenly. Atman kept taking notes, and only when the car would suddenly jolt did he cast a sidelong glance at Aramea, whose brown eyes he perhaps tried to catch.

I was becoming sleepy. I enjoyed keeping my head down. So the hills became more distant, and the treetops indistinct, as they blended with the faraway clouds. I was searching for a lost line, perhaps the lunar node or a vague development of suppositions and proposals that I could no longer coordinate.

I probably slept. When I rubbed my eyes to look, we were already near Palica. The landscape was changing, and the mountains began to stand out with a dense mixture of mounds and ridges studded with prickly pears. Gusts of rain were coming from the right.

"When will it stop?" asked Aramea.

"Soon," answered Salvat, frowning because of the unnerving play of the windshield wipers. "We're already in Làmia."

It was a land that emerged from fans of olive leaves against a background of unusual mist. The perimeter of the hills was far away; in fact, very far away and immersed in a sinking mass of clouds. One could not always see the almond groves, the rocky stretches or the ravines full of grass that formed strips of changing green. The first spring flowers, few in number, were scattered on the brows of the slopes in the most subtle of colors.

"Someone is waving at us," said the young woman.

"Oh," uttered my brother, stopping the car and, for a moment, blocking my view of the road. "It's Uncle Totosimic."

"So, you've arrived," the latter said. He got in and, bringing in a cool wave of air, sat down beside me.

The car started to move again with a hiss reechoed by brambles and by tuff quarries filled with fresh water.

One could see Qalat-Minaw up there, in a floating chaos of clouds that sent forth luminous patterns on the strips of trees.

"They've been waiting for you for quite some time," said Totosimic, wiping his wet hair with his hand.

"The road isn't very good," observed Salvat.

At the fork in the road, we veered left, and someone shouted from a car, "Hey, slow down!"

We had to maintain a reduced speed, always in perfect alignment with the side of the road.

"I've got to stop making these calculations," said Atman. "The jolts are so strong that my pen is scribbling on the sheets."

"There'll be plenty of time for that," replied Totosimic. "Besides, what good are they now?"

The countryside began to take on the appearance of a mountainous area, with frequent rocks covered here and there with clumps of capers. And every so often summits and chalky crests led to green vales.

"It's a good thing the road was paved," my brother commented.

I had not come to Qalat-Minaw for some time, so I was surprised to see young eucalyptus trees rising on the slopes, their boughs blurring the downpours, the heaps of stones, the brambles and the immense sky.

Following the many turns in the twisting road, we arrived halfway up the slope, where we came across an occasional peasant on an emaciated donkey, right in the middle of the winding clay paths that ended at the edge of town. Some cars were coming toward us, their horns blaring as they sprayed the sides of our Giulia with mud and dirt.

"You've arrived just in time," said Uncle Totosimic, lowering a window to let in a breath of air. And turning to me, he said,

"O Zephir, you didn't expect to take this trip, did you?"

I made no reply.

As we approached the first houses of Qalat-Minaw, we no longer saw patches of low, tender grass where the season's first white daisies sprouted. The ground in various spots had become uneven; it had sunk or risen with a dislocation of strata and rocks. The road skirting the town extended along cliffs and spurs upon which prickly pears inadvertently brought the eye down toward the valleys. At junctions in the road, some men would emerge and, seeing our car slow down, would say to themselves,

"They've arrived. They just had to come. A woman, one of their distant relatives, is with them too."

II

They were waiting for us at the house, there on the plateau, which progressively broadened toward the hill of the Castle. The wind from the lowlands reached the very summit of the town with oblique gusts that made the windowpanes on our balconies vibrate.

"Ah, there you are," said Abel, the visitor, as soon as he saw us go up the staircase inside, where two large vases had been placed on two small cutoff columns; they contained no plants, and their soil had recently been raked.

The room, which was not very large, showed signs of recent turmoil, with relatives and friends seated along the walls, which varied in color with the changing shade and light coming from outside.

"Come in," said Aunt Agrippa, still blonde despite her advanced age.

"Oh, you're here too," she added, turning to Aramea, whom she kissed on the back of the neck.

And Al-Hakim, approaching me, whispered,

"He passed away within a few hours. Your father, Donnanè, is no more."

My grandfather Michele embraced me, exclaiming,

"His body, locked in his past existence, is laid out in the next room. On his face can be read the signs of an endless flight from himself. It's as if he had escaped his own limits. But if you look carefully, you'll see his shadow on one of the walls."

My brother was looking for our mother.

"She's upstairs," explained Aunt Agrippa, as she sat with a shawl over her head next to the others. "We thought it necessary to consult the scholars."

We went upstairs. My mother, all bent with age, met us with pensive eyes and said,

"It happened. There's nothing you can do about it."

The table was still there in the middle of the room. With a slow gesture she pointed to the balcony, through which the silent movement of the sky reached us. Atman approached the small terrace without listening to my mother who, repeating herself frequently in contrast to her usual self, said to him, "It's useless. They're signs or celestial bodies that bring us endlessly from emptiness to emptiness."

"We'll see," echoed Atman.

We followed him—Salvat, Totosimic and I.

A short distance away, two eggs with fine, symmetrical red and black circles set off a corner of the terrace.

"It passed through here," commented Totosimic softly. "Let's go back in." We looked around. Water curves suddenly appearing and then disappearing underscored the horizon. And it seemed to us that on some of the roofs we could see small objects, in the usual array of colors, which gradually immersed into distant rain-bearing whirlwinds heading for the unreachable valleys beyond the town.

"This is going to develop into a big problem. I've sensed it," said Atman, carefully looking around and observing the silent swarming of objects that became more and more indistinct as it approached the arid Ereian plateaus.

"It happened," insisted my mother, covering her face for a moment with her wrap.

Atman suddenly spoke of a demon-bird, immobile places, diagrams, forces, men and abysses beyond the world. We went back in. My sister, Welly, had also come.

"Why lose yourselves in complicated calculations?" she said. "Let's go downstairs. They're waiting for us there."

We all went back down, except for Atman. We were received with mournful speech by those who had gathered there and who, huddling ever closer together, sought with sluggish gestures to overcome the inertia that bound them.

"Oh, here they are," they said when they saw us. And Abel, the visitor, approaching us, asked, "What do you intend to do?"

"It's still very confusing," answered my brother. We stood there motionless and silent, rarely looking at one another.

Uncle Pino, one of my father's brothers, entered unexpectedly and, removing his coat, said that what had happened was incredible and beyond our comprehension and that of everyone else in Qalat-Minaw; nevertheless, whether it was a question of a bird or not, clear signs had been left inside and outside the house. He also said that it was necessary to follow a path and find out who had left those unusual signs which, if arranged together sequentially, would allow us to discover a basic reason for it all.

He added that it was time to abandon the melancholy humors of mourning and our old ways of thinking.

Unwittingly, he transmitted his agitation to all those present and to my father's other four brothers, who had been summoned to draw up a program.

And so, Geber, Tirtenio and Orlando arrived. Totosimic, as we know, was already with us.

To our surprise, Uncle Pino showed us some small fragments clearly laminated with circular crystalline layers. He claimed to have found them on the first flowers of some sweet flags because of their vivid brilliance.

"Let me see," Grandfather Michele said to him, taking a crystal between his forefinger and thumb, and slowly smelling it. Then, putting it against the light, he gradually moved it away from his eyes. Seeing that it emitted different colors at regular intervals, he added, "I believe what we have here is calamine or orizon. What else could it be?"

The Arab, Al-Hakim, observed that we were off the track because fantasy, not springing from sound principles, makes one easily dismiss both perspectives and chimeras.

My sister, Welly, had called Atman and he had come immediately, walking as usual with his head bowed and one of his shoulders slightly raised. As soon as he was apprised of the matter, he did not get excited but observed that the two colored eggs and the stony particles were to be considered good clues for unraveling the tangled mystery. We should not lose our heads if we wanted to restore what we had lost with our father's demise. We must remember that no body ever tends to a state of rest; the more ordinary vision draws near to it, the more it reveals its frequent changes and vibrations. The effect is apparent when its particles become unbound and are transformed, each vibrating in chains of elements.

"That might be," said Al-Hakim without conviction.

Uncle Pino advised acting without hesitation and employing teams in the countryside to trace the bird's route. We would certainly be able to do so because we could find those little stones before the storms of the season would transform them into cinders or tereniabin vapors.

If that were to happen, we would not be able to recognize them.

This opinion prevailed, but the plan could not immediately be implemented given the complexity of this unusual situation.

There was enormous confusion. This, in part, was easy to understand and explain since it was not a question of delirium but of the search for a guideline that supposedly would help us unravel the knotty problem.

Since all of this did not convince me, I needed a few days to reflect upon and understand the thousands of unknowns that, after all, were essentially insignificant when compared to the infinity of things.

Nevertheless, Uncle Pino went off to search for volunteers who, divided into groups, were to comb the hills, the ravines, the hollows of tree trunks as well as certain underground passages under the brambles.

After having examined the fragments more closely, my brother, Salvat, observed that the smelly fumes and the variable luminosity of the crystalline material had perhaps permeated now half, now less than half and now more than half of the rocks and the animal and vegetable substances.

Before leaving us, my mother added,

"Let everything remain as it is. What happened, happened."

Her sister, Aunt Agrippa, said that we were trying to tread on paths of the arcane which would always escape our minds, unless we had recourse to falcate shadows and the celestial signs interwoven in the zodiac. Aramea was resting her head against a windowpane, her forehead dimly illuminating the great fall of raindrops.

All of my father's brothers had gone out to organize the scourings in all the lands of Qalat-Minaw, but perhaps it would not be easy to unravel the obscure mystery, given the misty clouds and the increasing rain that greatly altered the appearance of the countryside.

The best spot for mapping out the various itineraries to be followed in our exploration was the high ground of the Castle, where a multitude ready to follow us gathered very quickly.

Almost all of us were there.

We decided to divide up the area to be searched into five zones circumscribed by imaginary lines within which we were to determine the bird's route. My brother proposed that we record the various moments of the bird's flight in superimposable diagrams, but no one could pay any attention to him in that noisy confusion.

In any case, the team led by big Orlando was to go toward Qaltag, or southwest, and was to carefully examine Altiq, Pietrenere, Passomagnum, Camen and Violo, one squad exchanging information with the other as they proceeded.

Totosimic's team, better equipped to explore the ravines locked in connecting systems and in a convergence and divergence of olive groves, was to go toward Arcura. These groves looked to us like an empty, gray, floating mass because of the occasional stormy showers.

My uncle Geber's squad was to head for Nunziata. This area was less rugged, but one had to elude the snares of the many birds that bent the branches of the trees, filling them with a great tangle of feathers and a confusion of sweet songs that could deaden the senses.

Uncle Pino was to comb various areas which from Malvikin and way down along the torrent of the Wadi Hamm were suddenly transformed into streams issuing from the rocks. And he was to go farther up toward the highland of Qamut, an area rich in olive, pear, juniper and pistachio trees, as well as in lavender and catnip plants. There one could better feel the influence of the stars, which could cause sudden calamities and storms, or bring chaos to incorporeal elements. Furthermore, it was necessary not to allow oneself to be deceived by small shoots, buds and first flowers, or by trees that had still not flowered nor budded in certain cold hollows, right where the bird could have passed.

Finally, there was Tirtenio's team, which exhibited greater hesitation because it was supposed to head toward the most remote valleys of the Wadi Hamm, where everything was mysterious, even the humors of roots. Or it was to go farther ahead, toward Piana, where orange groves gave rise to fantasies because of their orderly arrangement, their fragrant blossoms or certain scintillating seeds that could fool the keenest eye or sap one's energy with the subtle fires emanating from the fruit and even from Mars.

It was not easy to form the squads, select the men, separate them and then reassemble them according to their tendencies to be calm, strong, rational or melancholy—characteristics that are very important in view of the many impediments that might hinder such a vast exploration, which involved the search for the above-mentioned glassy fragments. The latter could be confused with sprouts or early flowers, which, being tawny and black, made the changing surfaces of the waters deceptive.

Before starting the work, Grandfather Michele arrived wrapped in a shawl. We were not expecting him.

"Oh!" he exclaimed. "I didn't think so many people had already assembled."

"What do you want?" asked Tirtenio, who wanted to act swiftly.

The old man told us we were chasing ghosts because the enigma would always remain. He said that we would erroneously be going from one point of Qalat-Minaw's territory to the other, through zones broken up and devastated by the heavy showers; or that we would be foolishly pursuing the sun, the darkness and the moon; and that, instead of finding traces of the bird, we might not find anything but insignificant mustard seeds.

"You've always been like that," again objected Tirtenio.

But, shaking his head, the old man observed that our efforts would always remain feeble and mediocre, and that we would remain ignorant of the processes of nature, where everything has a purpose not easily ascertained. To resolve the mystery it would not be enough to examine common or wild thyme, or flowers and shrubs very different from one another not only because of their shoots, saps and leaves but also because of their colors that change from one moment to the next on account of the sidereal day or the way in which their fibers, branches and boughs (as well as their first, middle and last fruits) are arranged.

The men in the squads listened to him, uncertain as to what the old man was trying to say. Thank goodness our umbrellas were shielding us from the rain, since all this was taking place on the esplanade of the Castle, beneath which the town appeared like a mosaic of foggy images.

Grandfather Michele had not yet finished when, after a few moments of silence, he went under an acacia and said that arcane things have no feeling nor do they possess a body, except for what is enough to make them imperceptible wandering essences. He also said that this happens in spring as well as in other seasons, during which they release their scents and dissolve, corrupt and submerge nature in chaos. The liver, he added, at that time wants to drink, and requires wine and water; the mind needs rest or stimulation; and sadness comes into being and spreads even to the snow that covers the mountains and hills.

"What are you saying?" retorted Totosimic, who had already furnished his squad with cloaks, sticks and hoes. "You're making us lose time. Don't you realize that?"

The old man, shaking his shawl to make the raindrops fall off, spoke to us of an al-tannur, of its fire and of the sapphire generated within it. He said that if such stones were to be found among the ashes, they might give us some indication as to how to resolve the intricate problem. It was also necessary to keep in mind that the moon could rescind the attraction of Mars and Venus and make their skies coalesce, as long as the growth of the other planets permitted it, because everything—men, air, fire, water—resides in the immense circle of the planetary systems. It is there that we should look for our secret, in the band of forces that attract one another like lodestones, sending forth corals and mysteries of different intensities even deep down in the earth, which feeds on a hotchpotch of scammony and its resin, and some rare putrescent flowers of the elder.

Atman was furious. He interrupted my grandfather, saying that his reasoning was a muddle in which the arcanum was a primordial force and an absolute monarchy. We, instead, should use all our faculties to elucidate the means, motion and properties (or their absence) of the bird's flight.

Grandfather added nothing more, and casually shaking the acacia's low boughs, walked toward a small gravel road. Mansur, the sage, as he was called, straightening up his lanky frame, said that the old man was right if one presupposed that the unexpected apparition of the bird was a transmutation of vital principles, so that a hepatic stone could become alabaster; flint, granite; and trees, with respect to their seeds, could receive impulses excessive to their growth; and, finally, that astral time could entail terrestrial time.

"Quiet!" shouted Tirtenio. "We have to act and not create fantasies!"

Rowley, holding his pipe in his hand, advised not letting ourselves be deceived in our search for the fragments by the variable luminosity of the objects under the rain, which spread around in small and extremely small drops that altered the appearance of things. He added, as his blond beard became even wetter, that the bird might be a form of cosmic life unknown to us, and that its flight might perhaps be taking place in primary or secondary paths toward the center of Qalat-Minaw's territories, to the west or to the east.

My brother ordered us to put an end to all these controversies since to discuss projects, suppositions and personal views implied a useless delay.

Totosimic agreed, telling us to start searching immediately, since it was useless to establish unproductive or unreliable principles from that point on.

Suddenly we heard some birds chirping, not all of them making the same sounds, and we saw rocks falling headlong from the ruins of the Castle.

"Hey, what's happening?" asked Orlando.

Three boys and two girls were clapping rocks and hands together obliquely.

"Hey, you!" Pino called out. "Where are you from?"

They laughed, gathering speed as they rapidly whirled down the sloping rocks. Then, collecting some small rocks, they threw them down the slope, and illuminated by the changing light of the clouds, they entered a hollow, saying one at a time:

"I'm Muslim."

"I'm Mariela."

"And I'm Gheorghy, the singer."

"And I'm Ziritia. Don't you know Ziritia?"

"Me, Emanuele! Can't you see?"

They went on imitating birds, but down there their singing faded, muffled as it was by piles of stones.

"Oh, look, oh, look," exclaimed Uncle Pino, smiling and slapping his hand against his pants.

"Why don't you come with us?" shouted my brother, Salvat. "You can help us in this crazy venture."

But they could no longer be seen.

"Let's go!" said Tirtenio.

Bethsam, a well-known hunter, said that we would find not one winged creature but a thousand of them, and that such an unlikely exploration should not be undertaken if we did not have at least one clue at our disposal. We paid no attention to him.

Atman went back to apprise himself of the conclusions of the scholars and astrologers, who were supposed to arrive from the summits and shadows.

"So long," he said. "Good luck in your work."

Water was dripping down from the edges of our umbrellas, which annoyed us a bit. There were three paths that led down from the hill. Each group chose one of them, going silently among the reddish crags and the low swarming leaves that were clearly arranged in equal groupings and were all of the same size.

III

The solutions suggested did not convince me, but I kept silent so as not to upset the others. I decided only to extract the common denominator from the searches and observations to be made by each band as they industriously traveled about the countryside for many rising miles under watery vapors that tired the eyes, which had to look up in the mixture of humors and shadows.

At first I followed Totosimic's squad, which, among other things, was better prepared to satisfy the ardent desires of the men who, from one group to another, took leave in subdued voices.

For a while, we went along with Orlando and his proselytes, but after the Washhouse, we left them to enter a ravine whose unsymmetrical paths led to Sanmargher, a putrid, marshy land, where we trudged through the mud that, despite ourselves, clung to our shoes.

"The most suitable zone to cross is that of Azdrak," said Bethsam, the hunter. "It's probable that the bird went through there." But Totosimic said that that was not the course to follow, that is, that we should not limit the past events to the foolish movements of feathered animals, and he advised going northward to find the caves from which plumes of smoke in the shape of very white cubes shoot up over the mountains.

Let's not engage in false reasoning," answered Bethsam.

For the most part we encountered rain-drenched olive trees full of early blossoms, heaps of clods that we crumbled with our hoes, or hot streams that made millipedes, spiders and other insects suddenly come out of growing roots or moldy dust.

Once in a while someone would stop to look around attentively in case something unforeseen or scaly emerged.

With us was old Abdfilip, a great connoisseur of the valley since he had worked there for many years. His advice was useful to us even if sometimes, when he was in a bad mood, he would say that that land had offered, and still now in part offers, rich harvests, flowering meadows and rows of olive trees winding up hillocks; and, therefore, that a bird certainly seeking other air currents, other stars and perhaps even the night, could not have passed through there.

Fortunately for us, such outbursts were rare, and Abdfilip helped us unselfishly, especially when he took off his cap and scratched his bald head to help us resolve our doubts.

Soon we were down near the gorge of the torrent, which suddenly became swollen with rather noisy waters. It was an area full of prickly pears and agaves.

As soon as we passed the conical mouth of the torrent and were on the first clay steps leading to Azdrak, Bethsam pointed to a shiny fragment, possibly a chip of flint or a bit of the same sort of material left behind by the bird.

"Let's examine it," he said.

With a little digging he found two other similar objects. He vigorously hoed the ground in the vicinity; it revealed numerous fissures, oblique peaks and large holes that each of us interpreted his own way.

Despite losing over an hour digging furrows, looking at crests, damp rocky masses, tangles of worms and clear ponds, we only came to vague reflections and unfounded reasons concerning the bird's route.

We started climbing again. There were more and more trees, and in contrast to how I had imagined them, they cast faint shadows on the outcrops of the hills.

The olive thicket was still and silent.

"We should beat against some trees," advised Bethsam. "Something might be hidden in their hollows."

Because of that new task, sounds reverberated from one tree trunk to another, losing themselves in the intervale. We heard a whirr.

"Let's stop," whispered Bethsam, the hunter.

Totosimic smiled and said that the true substance of visible lands was composed of colors and vibrations, nor could it hide wooden elements or the filthy droppings of the thanatobird.

A bird above us slowly opened its wings and tried to decrease their flapping so as to escape the sudden appearance of the men mirrored for an instant in the sphere of sun.

"It's got to be brought down!" cried Bethsam.

"Don't kill it," suggested Abdfilip. "That wouldn't make any sense."

The bird, in a frenzied ascent, kept on a path that was not at all elusive or enigmatic.

Bethsam riddled one of its wings with a single shot. The wing broke and no longer flapped, so that the bird lost altitude as it tried to reach the sources of the stream, where it sought refuge in a secluded area feebly illuminated by night-wandering lights.

It was unable to continue much longer. It glided continuously lower, superimposing its feathers and becoming entangled in the highest branches until it was forced to rest on the ground.

Good for you, Bethsam," someone said. "You're a perfect shot."

They seized the bird, which had ruffled its feathers as soon as they approached it. And old man Abdfilip, with a shrewd smile, tersely said,

"It's an owl. What were you expecting?"

Totosimic in turn said,

"It's a mobile indication of what is moving from east to north."

Meanwhile, it stopped raining, and a sickle of light enveloped the slope, revealing a sparse flowering of plants. We saw the vegetal mantel covering the mountain's gray flanks and lava flows from top to bottom. Verdant bulbs and kernels of wheat emerged from the damp clay, visibly molding the ditches.

Bethsam advised hanging the owl by one of its claws so that its cry would serve to attract other birds. He enjoyed making a slip-knot with a small cord with which he tied the owl, that quickly emitted a sad sound among the bushes.

"*Ga-gaar, ga-gaar, ga-gaar, ga-gaar, ga!*"

Old Abdfilip continued to talk. He said that nothing could hurt the other bird, which was not the sort that we would find, but was a flying flame linked to the node of Pisces, into whose destiny we were attracted together with the water coming from the mountains and the seas.

No one answered him. We again continued climbing in the scaly clay terrain through the occasional plains that suddenly appeared. All the while we praised and blamed ourselves for the venture we had undertaken, until we stopped under a crag from which rainwater poured out copiously.

We had to decide whether to continue the exploration or stop at the homes of some peasants, because it was almost nightfall. The peaks of Arcura were farther up, and there was little daylight left.

Meanwhile, we were joined by Lucrezio, the carpenter, a messenger of my uncle Pino. He told us that great progress was achievable in his parts, given the many clues that we could discover by traveling through there, and the thousands of routes taken in infinite ways by the thanatobird—through almond groves, brambles and celestial places.

"Everyone has his own opinion!" observed Totosimic.

In the meantime, we continued down a rocky path in the hope of reaching some plateau where we could rest.

Bethsam, turning to Abdfilip, maintained that we should not put a great deal of stock in flights of thought about rare creatures whose existence cannot easily be verified. Instead, we should pursue all species of non-migratory birds in the lands of Qalat-Minaw, which, after all, could be reduced to only a few vagabond sparrows, ravens, partridges, nocturnal birds holed up in mysterious shelters and sparrow hawks disturbed by the rain. It was therefore useless to study the apparently insignificant diversity of the other winged creatures. In his opinion, we would find their shapes and molds in some old putrid nests, in moving shadows, in solitary cries. As regards the motion of the birds, one of which could have been ours, it was necessary to sketch and map out the areas we would cross. Nor did he believe that we were dealing with disease, fog or an empty buzzing body but rather with a common flying creature similar to the shrike, the woodpecker, the merlin, the blackbird and, who knows, if not to the bluejay or the mistlethrush (that feeds on ivy), or to the starling, the warbler, the golden-crested wren and even to the oriole, the cuckoo or to other songbirds.

We let him talk because the tasks we had performed had exhausted us.

Fortunately, we came upon a group of houses still inhabited by the few peasants who lived up there cut off from the world. One of these peasants, named Omar, was marking on the trunk of an olive tree some hacks that were supposed to represent the sun moving away and the approaching shadow which contracted and became dense in the bushes.

"Hey, what are you looking for?" he asked when he saw us.

Totosimic said that we were hunters, and Bethsam nodded in agreement, then immediately asked him to put us up for the night. The old man was hesitant, but when he recognized Abdfilip, he invited us to enter the large room on the ground floor where he lived.

Many of our companions dispersed to the other houses with the reciprocal promise to continue the hunt at dawn if it would finally stop raining, while I was to reach Pino's encampment in the valley of the Wadi Hamm. Omar told us that he could offer us cooked broad beans served in oil.

They were already cooking in a pot placed on two large stones against the wall on the right. And the aroma spread around pleasantly, descending down the slope toward a canebrake. His daughter, her hair already white, got some bowls ready. Her father stirred the pot very slowly with a wooden spoon as it came to a boil. The woman clarified the vinegar, both the white and the red, to make the dish more tasty, and meanwhile asked us whether we had killed beccaficos, swifts, larks or turtledoves, which she would gladly season with fennel flower and salt, and cook on skewers with small pieces of lard alternating with bay leaves.

"No," answered Bethsam. "The day didn't go well for us."

"It doesn't matter," said Omar, first serving Abdfilip, who, having sat down on the floor cross-legged, asked for some onions and bread.

We did the same. Omar looked out the door, observing that the color of the horizon was becoming perceptibly black because it was almost nightfall.

Out of a backpack we took some cheese, biscuits and pieces of bread with jam.

"Put them back," said the old man.

We slowly ate the well-cooked broad beans, the bread and the onions, while Omar, pointing his finger at the roof, observed that the nocturnal revolution and the conjunction of the planets had begun under the distant mountain of Arcura.

Then, sitting down in front of a blazing crimson fire in a circle of stones, he came out with a rigmarole that he perhaps often repeated to himself and to his daughter, Zyiàd.

"Now," he said, "what we have here is not broad beans but eggs fried in various ways, sauteed escargots smothered with sauce, small shrimps, mackerel served with slices of small lemons, and spinach browned and seasoned with rose-colored vinegar."

His daughter was nodding her head with damp eyes and arrested the motion when her father occasionally paused.

"But all this is not enough for our gentlemen. There's also grilled kid stuffed with sweet basil; there are cheeses, spices, capon breasts, veal osso buco and sausage laced with fat. And, at this point, to avoid the soporiferous humor, or to make it stronger and more pleasurable, I will offer you various kinds of yellow quince jam, cups of pomegranate seeds, sweet fennel, rosolio and sweet-smelling wines, while my daughter, Zyiàd, will bind your feet with threads of gold and silk. And let the wind blow outside and let the rain fall!"

IV

A few days later I left Totosimic and went with Bethsam and Abdfilip to the valley of Azdrak. It did not take us long to get there since we took some shortcuts that, winding along a path full of wormwood and hawthorn bushes already in bloom, brought us to where my uncle Pino had pitched his tents for the night.

"Welcome," said Mansur, the sage, stretching out his arms and pointing to the vast areas they had explored.

This low-lying plain, where the wheat was quite high and had a sprinkling of bluebottles, seemed to them to be an important element of the event in question.

"Oh, look!" said Pino.

The design of the leaves was not parallelinervate as usual but was broken up into curvilinear fibers which were especially numerous toward the center of the field.

Abdfilip, an expert in such things, winced and observed that strange things such as these stem from the visual sense and do not add much to the phenomena to be examined when we came across less evident things throughout the universe of Qalat-Minaw—a universe shrouded in a chaos of clouds, newly sprouted grasses, olive trees and streams formed by the rainy spring season.

However, there were some who thought at first that they had found the key to the mystery.

Rowley, for example, said that this zone was to be considered a nodal point especially since Pino spoke to him of fragments of striated shells which could be found, with a little patience, in certain concentric circles in the rocks. It was not easy to judge the matter impartially, and everyone set forth their reasonings and complex arguments to support their own opinions.

Mansur, for example, suggested examining all the different forces that emerged in the field of our apparent knowledge, and looking not so much for small signs, false fortuitous causes, but for very hard primitive material that was multipliable and reducible to musical elements, or to sentient bodies that uninterruptedly filled the voids of the valley.

Yahin, small and swarthy, proposed, with his good sense, that we return to town and to what had always been, letting actions, wheat harvests, mysteries and slimy filth follow their incongruous game outside our daydreams.

"What in the world are you saying?" retorted Pino, his white hair wet from the raindrops falling from the trees. "Our journey begins here. You'll see that we'll explain every paradox."

Atman had also come and was rather upset because controversies were arising so easily. Even Al-Hakim, Aunt Agrippa's confidant, did not delay in joining the group. To justify his presence, he had brought along young Aramea, who sat astride his horse, her face partially covered by a veil.

"Who asked you to come?" inquired Uncle Pino.

Al-Hakim replied that this was not the time to hesitate but to look for still other forms or clues; and that would not be difficult if we turned our eyes to the surrounding almond groves in bloom.

"What do you mean?" asked Yahin.

Aramea had gotten down and was looking at all of us and the undergrowth of broad beans whose black-speckled inflorescences became one with the bright strips of wild flowers slightly hidden by the falling rain. Al-Hakim answered that it was time to turn our attention to the nests already present on the branches, to buds or to the crowns of trees, rather than to the rifle shots of hunters lost on the heights.

"It's not a bad idea," Pino remarked. "We could profit by that. Every trace could be useful to us."

Abdfilip nodded his head at the thought that the almond groves of the valley of Azdrak could be reduced to the essential web of fronds and shrubs composing the entire flowery band.

At that moment we heard some branches shaking not far away, and some very light petals moved about in the air, forming a white spiral.

"What's that?" shouted Lucrezio, busily examining several tree trunks with the palms of his hands.

We turned around. From the white clump of almond trees we saw some eyes watching us with intense curiosity and doing all they could not to be noticed.

"Who are you?" exclaimed Yahin.

Pino laughed, having recognized Muslim, Emanuele, Mariela, Gheorghy and Ziritia.

"You've come just in time," he said. "Knock down the flowers so that we can find the bare structures of the nests."

"Oh no," said Yahin. "What sense is there in wasting the harvest? Let's catch the children."

"Let's stop them," added Abdfilip. "Let's leave the plants to their fate."

The children, seeing that they were discovered, and realizing that they were the target of various intentions, made their way among the branches of the treetops, and in so doing accidentally broke off tender leaves and scattered all around a cloud of petals that spun high in the air and onto the slope of the valley. With that, the countryside below was overshadowed not only by the downpours or the clouds coming from the southeast but also by the collision of almond blossoms whose colors, as Rowley specified with a sardonic grin, flew about in the air with trillions of vibrations per second.

The five children, believing they were being pursued, leaped from tree to tree, all the more excited by Yahin's shouts of "Stop! Stop!" and they destroyed much of the soft coverings provided by the flowers. They appeared and disappeared among the airy treetops, whose shapes changed from moment to moment. Meanwhile, Aramea had gone off some distance and, sitting down on the trunk of a felled tree upon which moss had begun to form, looked at the dense, expanding cascade of floral remains and suddenly plunged into them as they glistened and spiraled about her. Al-Hakim was watching her. She extended her arms and waved her hands gently about in that soft, unstable mass, and, I believe, she untiringly gazed eastward, calling Yusuf in a low voice, even though, as we know, he was far away. Then, with a quivering voice, she evoked the presence of her beloved in that adventitious shower of petals.

When Emanuele climbed down from the trees, he discovered in the bare structures of the almond trees several recently-started nests made of spirals of hay, feathers and fibers. He collected them to please Uncle Pino and Al-Hakim, who thought they would find mysterious signs and traces of the bird's passage in them. Aramea picked one up at random. It was perforated and unfinished. After brushing it with her hair, she raised it with her hands stretched out toward the impenetrable circle of the horizon, which faded in the celestial sphere amid slow-moving, nascent clouds.

Atman looked at her from atop a rock, his face lit up by the motion of multiple lines traced by the falling flowers. With darting eyes, he tirelessly gazed at her shape, which seemed to project itself, because of the above-mentioned cloud of sepals and pistils, on an ever-changing screen composed of young wandering birds and embryonic nests. He came down toward me slowly and, taking me aside, told me that all these phenomena before us appeared to him in contradiction to the very rain and the very winds that the thanatobird supposedly brought. In his opinion it was therefore necessary, instead, to seek the bird in the igniferous heavens of the solar system or in a quantity of extraterrestrial atoms.

I looked at him apprehensively at first and walked along with him under the trees of an almond grove that extinguished the muted cries of the children as they traveled from tree to tree toward higher ground. Then he told me that it was not enough to study the billions of helium corpuscles, but that it was perhaps necessary, if nothing came from our operations, to graft a small human being onto a branch of an olive or some other tree so that its animal-vegetal nature could give us some clarification regarding the bird's action on the graft's hybrid growth.

I remained silent, not knowing what to answer him, who at this point spoke softly, making only slight allusions to the graft.

Farther ahead, the men were looking up, right in the middle of the woods where the nests with their indefinite oval shapes stood out, filtering the sight of the passing gray clouds.

"Now what?" said Yahin. "All we've done is cause damage, and we can't reattach the buds and the very small fruit that will end up taking oxygen from the puddles."

The bluffs, sketched by a dripping wet mass of dead branches and by thick waves of terrestrial vapors, seemed quite barren. Abdfilip weighed in his hand the few nests that had barely been started and that someone handed to him. He strung them on long sticks and counted them as he arranged them in parallel rows on the turf.

Aramea, sensing that she was being watched, had leaned against an olive tree with her ear on the bark as if she were trying to capture subtle underground vibrations or fragments of scales that would absorb the momentary luminous rays.

"Come now," said Pino disconsolately. "We've got to extend the search. The meager data that has been collected and the bizarre scale of nests that Abdfilip has arranged on the ground are not sufficient."

In fact, they were the common works of brooding birds: wisps of feathers and lichens, and concave remains of ordinary substances.

Atman did not express his thoughts to everyone, but he left us, saying that it was time for him to prepare a great number of calculations up there in Qalat-Minaw, and that the scholars would be a great help to him in the search for the general effects of the entire affair. He advised us to go down through the wooded slope and not lose sight of the centrifugal motion of the "fireball," which had certainly not stopped in a restricted area but had probably gone beyond the confines of our territories. Being an infinite power, it could move one or one hundred thousand verdant grains, and for a larger circular movement could effect an entire rotation under the lunar wings.

"Goodbye," said Pino as soon as he saw him fade out of sight among the sorghum and hawthorn bushes.

"So be it," he then concluded. "Let's proceed farther down."

And so we walked along the Malvikin crest in a mountainous area where it was easy to find deformed seeds and flowers growing in irregular formations, until we heard the noise of the Wadi

Hamm, whose powerful purple waves followed the riverbed in its southerly course.

"This way," advised Abdfilip, as he pointed to a path flanked by broom plants. Aramea and Al-Hakim had followed us, attracted, I believe, by the messages that seemed to be coming from the moon that night. But the young girl was not happy, even if she managed on her own to wriggle out of tufts of wet grass, rocks and renascent thorny thistles.

Since it was late, we stopped at an abandoned house on the edge of a ravine near the river. Aramea preferred to stay in a hut made of reeds and straw, not very far from our own place of refuge.

The rain decreased, becoming intermittent, even though with great sudden downpours that resounded throughout the olive groves. And then Al-Hakim gave us a message from Aunt Agrippa, who had been unable to reach the valley not so much because of an infection on her right knee but because of her advanced age. Sitting cross-legged in the middle of Pino's group, he told us calmly that it was not sufficient to follow Atman's advice concerning the rising of the moon, which anyway would not be visible if the rainy conditions continued to prevail, nor was it sufficient to examine the lights or shiny ravelings that the moon emits in bands of magnetic collisions, or the impossible changes in the lunar orbit, since they were an illusion caused by the clouds that traveled through the fog and the vaporous jets of the valley. On the contrary, to resolve the mystery and better receive the celestial signals, we needed the colors white, silver and lilac to purify the chosen spot from terrestrial exhalations. Since our satellite was waxing, Al-Hakim collected some peonies (which, fortunately, were available), and these, together with pearls and agates, were to further clarify the shadow of the crevice on the moon, which was traveling southwesterly in the sky, and which would perhaps indicate the route of the bird—a very useful thing if we made some effort to discover it. And in this he was in agreement with Atman.

Pino, who was upset, asserted that it was only up to him to explore that stretch of lands where so many extraordinary realities converged.

"We ought to go ahead," he said, "climb up to Qamut and not waste our time pursuing sidereal illusions."

But his advice served only to vent his feelings because he could not counter the arguments of Atman and the scholars, and the ones communicated by Aunt Agrippa through less conventional means, all of which counseled not ruining the entire operation that we had undertaken.

Fortunately, when evening came, it did not rain as much as we had thought it would, and Abdfilip himself, looking up, exclaimed that the inverse movement of the clouds was about to end, since the sky was rather clear in the area around Pozzillo. The sky over Qamut turned bright with no cloudy masses. We heard the chirping of a cricket, an omen of fine weather. Sitting outside under a shelter made of branches, we waited for the heavenly body to rise. Many of us were dozing when Yahin said: "The peasants will have a good harvest this year."

And Pino:

"That's all you think of!"

Rowley even wanted to follow the hourly lines of the luminous rays, and to this end marked the rock in several spots in order to have a sort of descending scale of lunar movements. Meanwhile, the moon made the countryside appear swollen and wet with a network of very minute quivers that slowly increased in the tree trunks, branches and hedges.

Then, unexpectedly, we heard a soft lullaby coming from Aramea's hut. Aramea was singing to her sleeping baby, brought from Qalat-Minaw in a basket covered with iris buds.

"What's happening?" asked Yahin, nodding his head from sleep.

Lucrezio had climbed an almond tree to better hear the singing that changed from soft to loud with sudden pauses and amorous trills that gave it countless plaintive tones there, outside, in the streaming lunar plasma which spread in luminous patterns on our faces and on the rugged rocky paths. Al-Hakim and Rowley did not remain idle. The latter looked for numerical relationships in the rays that the firmament was sending us in silent movements. And the former, the Arab, burned dried peony leaves, whose smoke intermingled with sparkling minerals, raindrops still lingering in the air and traces of clouds.

A few words reached us from the hut:

"Diofar, ia ibn El Asari—scebihoun bil tair—moharrir Al sharr min alalam, iesch Al naim Al shafik—allathi al saad minhu, edilhu—yalli qorb al nom—man yara fi al mal yegri alayhi..."

Abdfilip told us that Aramea was rocking her baby boy, who had never been seen by anyone, and was calling him "dove," "liberator of evils" and "sleepy one." She was doing so next to a well where the motion of the bucket relaxes and induces sleep in whoever looks at it as it trembles in the dark water it draws.

The lullaby continued with an alternating rhythm and rose up the flanks of the valley. It now no longer seemed an extraneous variation of the night. On the contrary, because of the changing rain covers still visible in the direction of the Catanan plain, it incited us to observe the infinitesimal layer of lunar dust descending from up above. And many of the men in the squad had the impression that the ravines nearby were no longer what they had thought they were but rather a mixture of titanium, beryllium and iridium which, refracting in different tonalities, tripled the vibrations of the light.

Rowley was the one who was the most misled. He roused those lulled to sleep by Aramea's lullaby and said that the absorption and the contemporaneous emission of radiating substances from small dark fissures, from bumpy and encrusted surfaces and from the varying sounds of rustling leaves corresponded—according to his careful analysis of the particles and the bewitching sounds that the young lady employed in coaxing her baby to sleep—to trillions of oscillations per second.

"I'm talking to you!" he puffed, as he walked among us to keep us awake and make us follow him in the algebraic enigma he was trying to explain. "If you pay attention and don't follow the trivial dimensions of the present, all you have to do is sever the rays of the lunar band that is about to paste itself with unusual brilliance on the young girl's hut and that is blazing forth above it like a luminous pinnacle, and you will notice that we are not dealing with the color white or with the seething of waves, but with four hundred and forty trillion vibrations per second of the color red, one thousand and more of the color orange, and one thousand six hundred and sixty vibrations of yellow elements."

"What in the world are you saying?" countered Uncle Pino, as he stood erect on the edge of a rock and sniffed the smells that were widespread in that area and that came from the fissures in the river or from the fluvial grasses lapped by the current.

Fair-haired Rowley continued to rattle off figures and vagaries about colored numbers without anyone paying any particular attention to him. Noticing this, he purposely shook some almond trees to make us feel our absentminded clumsiness and notice the extremely minute corpuscles that were divisible in an endless chain and that permeated our eyes and ears, open in that moment only to Aramea's singing and her demure image.

Al-Hakim finished burning the arboreal ingredients, which some of us sniffed with pleasure. Leaving the embankment, he said in his low, persuasive voice that Rowley was talking nonsense, closed as he was in a confusion of numbers and infinitesimal vibrations of time. He further said that Rowley did not note, as one could well see, that the Wadi Hamm was enshrouded by seven spheres floating within a continuous fall of souls governed by the very distant whirl of the planets.

"Oh, what in the world are you saying!" reechoed Yahin. "Can't you see that the low-lying waters remaining on the lands are enriching the harvest of the few peasants who have not yet emigrated?"

Fortunately, the young girl gradually stopped her singing, and suddenly, one could say, desires and hopes quieted down. Rowley did not wish to repropose explanations and verifications of primary and concomitant causes, and Al-Hakim stood there, his arms raised toward the heights, and immediately went away as soon as he saw my brother, Salvat, arrive from a side road, avoiding branches bent by the weight of their buds.

"What do you want at this late hour?" Uncle Pino asked him.

Salvat said he had come to tell us about what had been discovered up there at Qalat-Minaw regarding the explorations conducted by the other groups.

"It's time to sleep," concluded Pino. "Let's restore our strength with sleep. Tomorrow you can tell us about what happened."

Before we fell asleep on the straw in the abandoned house, Salvat, stretched out near me, told me in a whisper that he had considered another aspect of our venture but did not want to speak to anyone about it. He explained that, first of all, he did not want to worry our mother, who silently went from room to room, resting only at dawn. Secondly, he did not want to worry our sister, Welly, who, convinced that the rapidly passing days would extinguish the sorrow we felt for our father and put an end to the investigative activities of the groups, might become alarmed and undertake a secret maneuver, who knows if with anger or good spirit, overturning every plan. And thirdly, it was better that everything ended as it had come to be, steeped in doubts and vain opinions.

When I delicately asked him what he meant (everybody was sleeping, and not a sound came from outside), he told me we would never resolve our fears and passions nor would we find assurance and peace of mind until we examined the semblances of our father's remains.

V

And now I will briefly discuss the deliberations of the other groups and the results they obtained during those few days, and I will tell about the sublime, mistaken or controversial conclusions that they arrived at in the course of their travels.

After coming down the slope of Pietrenere, Orlando went toward Qaltag, often along sandy strips of land covered with capers, in an area where there were stretches of gravel and clay. I cannot tell you in detail how he combed the agreed zones, at the same time we all did, to arrive at Làmia, where he was to meet Tirtenio.

In fact, in some respects, the two squads occupied adjacent territories, but in branching out radially in a centrifugal manner, they went in opposite directions, farther and farther away from each other.

Among other things, the squads had their own homogeneity because of the criteria they used in selecting their men, who obviously had to have particular qualities to deal with the knowns and unknowns of the various territories.

Orlando and Tirtenio were similar in that they both related their experiences of the exploratory trip with the same calm objectivity. They had preferred to choose individuals who, though pervaded by doubts, relied on sound deductions that enabled them to overcome terrible fears that might arise from erroneous presumptions concerning the divine and the continual regeneration of sprouts or diaphanous quartz among the schists. Moreover, they were rather well-groomed and clean-shaven. They had short hair with sparse curls drenched from the rain which had fallen almost continuously from the rapidly swirling clouds. (All this is said for the common reader who is probably perplexed.)

However, since these men were poorly combined, they would have produced a system of analysis and research that could have become essentially destructive had it been taken as an end in itself.

But there being an apparent *ubi consistam* to discover, possibly within a short span of time if they were not to lose essences and important traces, the men were to express their convictions and preferences freely (and in this Atman and the scholars were in agreement). If these things were discussed and sublimated with no regard to hunger, thirst and sudden cold, they would have brought results of exceptional validity. Unfortunately, among the men (as one might have foreseen) there was no lack of "diehard skeptics" ready to grapple with dilemmas and the greatest rituals of worry concerning the meaning of life and the demon-bird, or tenaciously attached to the all too obvious limits of daily living and the meaning of heaven and Hades. But this concerned only a small number of individuals who could easily be swayed.

Let us now consider the results obtained, which, as always, were uncertain because of chance factors and the very short time during which they were achieved.

Orlando, after having left behind the above-mentioned area of Pietrenere, reached the "plain" in two days, heading toward Qaltag, a large town that one could see on mountainous overhangs, with black houses alternating with white ones. In those lands, the orange groves did not have the vigorous growth they had on the opposite slope. And roaming about in the night were intense stars, long, hornlike trails of fog rising from the undergrowth, some birds frightened by passing cars, and slow shadowy figures that resumed their former shapes after shaking slightly.

In that fleeting activity, everyone thought that by close examination he would find order and principles that would relate directly to the dreadful passage of the "fireball." For example, Mamhùd, a member of Orlando's team, considered it important that, if one looked carefully, one could see the branches of the orange trees, still laden with their last fruits, bending eastward, perhaps having been left that way purposely by the peasants. He also maintained that a mysterious force with millions and millions of ergs had also acted in that fertile region. On the basis of conjecture, he even interpreted the bubbles of gas expelled at night by the frogs, whose uninterrupted croaking in artificial ponds and natural puddles sharpened vigilant hearing.

After following the route through Sanmargher, Totosimic took a solitary path that led up to Arcura, where, because of the chaotic growth of the trees, night fell rapidly, acquiring blackness without passing through the infinite degrees of sunset. He did not stay there but continued with his men toward Nunziata, a pleasant zone that was easy to cross, with centenary olive trees that opened to the sun from the very first hours of the day.

They paid close attention to small stones, fossil shells embedded in rocks, clods that had grown green again, birds that repeatedly flew around gnats, and to rays reflected from the water in the ditches.

Totosimic was convinced that these findings and signs were ambiguous, and he reproached Attanasio, his helper, for relying on preconceived notions and symbols and, what is worse, for arousing many suspicions in the men of his group. Then he spoke of the cave that faces north where, though a climate suitable for vegetation was absent, furrows and frozen lakes appeared which contained coagulated seeds that generated things.

We learned from Rowley what had happened to the squad of Tirtenio, who had the wisdom to select:

1. a number of "melancholics," forming about 30% of the total. These men, *tenues et breves et nigri*, were moved by contrary causes, fearing but also believing in myths and thinking that there may not be feeling in death. They meditated frequently and almost motionless, being *solitudinem amantes*. Nevertheless, they thought that fluxes had been exchanged between the hypothetical bird and the three sorts of movements of the earth, the moon and the plants—things that indirectly followed the above-mentioned shifts, immersed, as they were, with rocks and waves, in celestial whirlpools;

2. a number of individuals commonly called sanguines, about 70% of the total, who, as you well know, are *bonae spei et boni ingenii et jucundi*. These men were scarcely at all disturbed by weaknesses, fears and the need for others, so that, not being prone to scepticism or irony, they reconciled their reasoning with the uncertain variance stemming from the fall of rocks, the humid blossoming of flowers and the occasional rains.

The route to Pozzillo was not easy, because of the many boulders that blocked the valley of the Wadi Hamm, the bats that, coming out of the labyrinths of rocky crevices, invaded the lands, and the many sudden obstacles posed by small, rapid torrents. Nevertheless, they reached the broad plain, where luminous lentisks, young olive trees and rain-drenched lemon trees turned into beautiful spirals of dazzling clarity.

Rowley maintained that billions of baryons deposited by the destroying ball in countless fertilized fields had swarmed through the ravines and through the fields of arid stubble.

We, the members of Pino's squad, listened to all of this, sitting out in the open near the grotto, from whose entrance capers and sassafras branches were hanging. And, according to that same account, a veritable scuffle and a lengthy argument with strongly disputed positions broke out among Tirtenio and the other men when toward evening the moon appeared over Etna, which, despite the encroaching darkness, could be seen in the distance with its slightly prismatic structure. At the site where they had stopped, there were numerous small houses abandoned by the peasants; and, though many of the sanguines only wanted to refresh themselves and fall asleep, the melancholics seated on the trunks of the trees, and several even on the roofs that were easy to reach, plunged into serious meditation.

As the orbiting moon rose higher and higher, illuminating the shores, the mainland, the rivers and the hills, those who were awake, burdened by sad humors, let their heads drop ever more down to their breasts. Instinctively they sought rest in the shade of the umbrellalike trees, some asserting that, being stricken by hundreds of thousands of lunar corpuscles coming from above, they felt even their exterior shapes changing.

Mansur observed that there was nothing exceptional in this account, since the transposition of atoms from the air to the ground and vice versa, measurable if one wished in regular systems, united the vegetal fluids better, changed weights and heights and, descending into the meanders of the soul, reduced the threads of serenity and multiplied the nodes of sorrow. He added that it would be better to stay in the meadows, playing instruments, eating, and looking for the first asphodels.

Rowley told him in reply that many of Tirtenio's men had covered their faces with leaves when they saw the shadow of the moon extend over the stones and the residual rainwaters near the Wadi Hamm.

Mansur observed that that was natural, since the almost total absence of peasants, who had definitively gone to other regions, gave to the common features of nature and to ourselves a greater sense of the transmutations because of the indistinct materials falling from the sky and emerging from the underground streams of liquid metals.

Uncle Pino went away, saying that it was time to put an end to useless discussions about unresolved problems. Approaching the river and pushing aside small branches and flowers drooping on their stems, with his finger he amused himself by playing with the waters that reflected the early morning sun and the faint passing clouds as they overshadowed one another. And he murmured repeatedly,

"O wave that comes, o wave that goes, where are you taking me?" Meanwhile, Aramea had left her hut, which was hidden in the thicket of almond trees, and went around collecting snails, rootlets, moss and poppy buds. In this way she distracted herself from her worries, at the same avoiding us.

Al-Hakim joined her on the opposite embankment and asked her if she wanted to go back up to town with him and let Pino's group complete the exploration of the district.

Since solar dust had invaded the valley, dissolving in its path fleecy clouds and the misty mouths of ravines, the young woman decided to prepare a cradle for her infant, Diofar. Paying no attention to Al-Hakim, she climbed up a holm oak and, after using her hands to remove viscous encrustations, fronds and dense drops, tied two silk scarves to a couple of branches and made a hammock near the top of the tree.

"Hey, what are you doing?" asked Yahin.

Aramea said her son loved the sun and she knew this because his heart beat faster whenever this star came closer.

So on the holm oak she put Diofar, who was wrapped in many veils and a mat, and for quite a while she rocked him amid the treetop's tender mass.

Rowley was busy with his calculations. Walking continuously along the bank of the little river, swollen because of the recent rains, he constructed conjectures and ephemeral numbers unwinding in series and chains of lunar cadenzas. Aramea sat serenely on a fork of the holm oak and with graduated motions sent the hammock high and then low toward the tangle of interminable leaves that emitted fragrance, sudden shadows and a pleasant rustling sound.

Diofar probably fell asleep soon because Aramea varied and shortened the movements of the improvised cradle, which continued to trace a concave curve in the sunlight.

And when we saw the hammock swinging less and less from one moment to the next, we knew the young woman would come down.

Not everyone paid attention to her; some lit a fire to prepare their meal, and others collected bundles of firewood.

The treetop stopped moving, and we could no longer even see the arm of Aramea, who was probably curled up there where every vibration had ceased. Then Al-Hakim, following her with furtive glances, called her repeatedly from a large bare rock blackened with mold on one side.

I do not believe the girl slept, but nestled as she was within the bent branches, she probably was looking at the high orange crags or perhaps at the sloping surfaces of the sky.

Since many of the men called her, she reluctantly climbed down, telling us her baby needed her breath to sleep better.

"Oh, come on," exclaimed Al-Hakim. "How can you spend hours and hours up there?"

He advised her to amuse herself by watching the solar emissions piercing through the almond grove, or to follow him, if she wished, along the bed of the Wadi Hamm, since she too was obliged to stay with us, as was only proper, because of Donnanè's death.

"Besides," he added, "you should be happy because your Yusuf will be leaving the subterranean vaults, gunpowder and saltpeter and will soon be by your side."

And so the girl followed him timidly up along the torrent, which, though narrowing, accentuated the depth of the gorge.

"Come," Al-Hakim said to her. "It's all beautiful."

He stopped purposely in the vicinity of the bank and showed her the shoals that, whitened by the pebbles, hid silt, crabs and very fine gold dust.

"Oh look!" he exclaimed.

They went farther and farther away from us, toward a remote area known for its oak groves and fern thickets.

Aramea was attracted to these spots, where there was no useless dispersal of pebbly clearings nor excessive sunshine. On Al-Hakim's suggestion, she would even go down into the riverbed to push away tufts of horsetails and to look at her reflection in the water that, churning less, and in several spots slowing down where there were slight protrusions in the bank, descended to the valley.

She enjoyed putting her hand in the current and observing with wonder the first flowering of the very low banks and the sudden appearance of fish, like the roaches and the sneaky chub, which fearlessly swam around her finger, greened by the emerging grasses.

The Arab observed her and led her farther up to distract her from her son (and, I believe, in this he was in agreement with Aunt Agrippa). Throwing a few crumbs from his flat cake to the few starving pikes or to the black bass that chose the most diaphanous waves, he made her smile and indirectly reminded her that for them

Sicily was the "half-moon lost in the sea," the "island of their dreams" in the nights that descend on the ardent sunsets of the desert.

Moving from crag to crag, they lost all contact with us. Then Lucrezio, vainly selecting hollow trunks suitably oriented to create echoes with great resonance, called them at the top of his voice to tell them we were waiting for them. But no one answered. Moreover, the young lady had been distracted by the sudden appearance of the children (the timid Mariela, fleet-footed Ziritia, Emanuele, Gheorghy and the singer, Muslim), who were on a hill covered with acorns and meadow daisies, and who were racing ahead of her, marking the path of the Wadi Hamm with their rapid steps. She asked them,

"What are you doing?"

Muslim replied that they were looking for an eagle which had flown at a very great altitude the day before, but who knows if that was true? And they had Aramea and Al-Hakim follow them in the undergrowth of olive and oak trees, where some of them bit into the heads of hawkweed that stained Aramea's feet and clothes sulfur yellow.

In short, the woman followed the man toward Trezzito, and it seems she was ever more fascinated by the landscape and by the children, who were close to her for a long stretch. Ziritia was able, with a stick, to make minnows jump out of the torrent. The fish, forgetful of the water, breathed for a moment with open gills, only to suddenly dive again into the current.

Then Muslim, as the leader of the group, told the children to stop following the woman who marveled even at the eggs deposited by frogs under the stones or at some finch emerging from the brambles. At that moment Gheorghy, Mariela and Ziritia, jumping over a ditch, climbed up the bank and very quickly greeted her from the branches of oak trees, on which they imitated partridges and wild doves, disappearing—it's not clear into which direction.

But Al-Hakim managed to distract Aramea and calmly spoke to her of the different kinds of honey and wine produced on the island, comparing the wine that was bitter, full-bodied, aggressive and austere to that which was sparkling, feminine, mellow and mild.

It seems he brought her back to Qalat-Minaw after they made a small tour of lands that for the most part were at the bottom of small valleys. These were areas where wheat and broad beans grew spontaneously amid indefinite scents that adverse winds brought from heaps of gray stones and stretches of wet clay.

However, we were faced with another problem that made the venture complicated and distressing. According to what we learned, all five of the groups had mistakenly focused on phenomena in an area where there were few people because the farms and huts had been abandoned. To some, such as to Attanasio and Totosimic, all this did not seem important: it was an insignificant element of an order that paradoxically could appear changed by what had been found in our house and by the perennial rain that, except for a few intervals of clear weather, had relentlessly stricken our countryside for several days.

But the majority of us preferred the idea put forth by Atman and the scholars, who wanted to obtain an animal-vegetal creature of ambiguous shapes and substances. They thought this idea could, with a succession of comparisons, allay our doubts and dilemmas if we had the good sense (or bad sense, as Mansur said) of studying the perceptible fluctuations caused by the thanatobird in its occult flights. And Atman, who had again joined us on the same day in which Aramea had wandered away from us, advised us, while we sat plucking the blue and white blossoms of the caper to clarify our thoughts and worries in silence, to carry out the foregoing experiment. In his opinion, we would thus facilitate a rapid conclusion to our quest and perhaps succeed in breaking the chain which had harnessed us to an adventure that would end with everything being resolved and us enjoying the applause of our squads.

We had a difficult afternoon, I must confess, because of the different reactions of those consulted who spoke on the subject.

Rowley, as was to be expected, was fascinated by the idea, and so much so that he cried privately, deep in a grotto. He was happy because one could reform and renew an old natural order that knew nothing more than dawn and dusk, shining crescent-shaped horns and magnificent, rich lands laden with pollen.

Pino was quite dismayed and, allowing everyone to express his opinion, had gone to the torrent as if he wanted to ask the surface currents to help him make a choice and to direct his mind in these unknown fields. He repeated the well-known refrain: "O wave that goes, o wave that comes, where are you taking me?"

Lucrezio, until then seemingly interested only in aromatic wood for his carpentry, said that the project was good because, besides yielding lumber of excellent quality, it could also bring about the ebb and flow of wandering constellations. Abdfilip scratched his head, stating that in the span of only a few days he had forgotten that heat and cold, causing putrefaction, stimulate reproduction without it being necessary for us to have recourse to a graft, as was our intention, which could only result in the fleeting glimmers of a man-tree.

"But what are we getting at?" he asked.

But from the glint in his eyes we understood that he would soon accept the idea, if only to see a being of memory-fibers arise from the transplant that would be rejoined to us through a series of un-foreseen happenings.

Bethsam, who never ceased hunting birds, killing them wherever he could (even in their very nests), did not immediately understand the proposal since he was used to the visible world around him. Finally, he observed that we would be wasting more time because the firebird had to be of terrestrial origin and in itself was not at all monstrous and unthinkable. We should be patient and look for it again. It was useless, therefore, to create a mortal graft in our dense woods.

"We won't obtain anything," he concluded.

When asked for his opinion, Yahin said that we had not yet ac-cepted the fact that we were pursuing an illusion, and that a new transmutation to be introduced in the regular succession of events and in a system of infinitely subdivisible phenomena was utter non-sense.

We were standing under a tree, and from time to time the passing wind brought some occasional raindrops.

The only one who decisively opposed the idea was Mansur, the sage. According to him, we would not derive any new element from such an experiment since the luminous substance that falls from the stars, the motion of the clouds or the spiral of leaves-soul that we planned to create in the lush valley of the Wadi Hamm would not have disturbed nor deviated the contaminating atoms that the demon had brought to us all. What is more, he felt vexed and was moved at the thought that Atman and the scholars had almost certainly focused their attention on the very small unsuspecting creature presently asleep in a suspended hammock made of branches.

But it was not possible, he went on saying, to use Diofar to find an answer to our questions, to sacrifice him in a void where only thousands and thousands of concentric circles of vegetal matter could make him appear to us like the joyful image of a living thing, and to leave him there forever in dizzy forms punctually renewing themselves in the spring. And had we forgotten Aramea? She, day after day and night after night, would pursue her son through lands and seas, and no longer having a physical loving rapport with him, would transmit her dolorous breath to reptiles, plants and aquatic creatures.

Mansur also spoke of our memory as having disintegrated, and of our frenzied search for a bird never seen before. But the men left him to his assertions and travails, and he, feeling lonely, conversed with the pebbles and gravel of the torrent.

As soon as we concluded that meeting, we saw three men arrive who greeted Atman with a smile.

"Here they are," the latter said.

Nergal, or Drop-of-blood as they called him, perhaps because of the slight bloody purpling at the corners of his eyes, was doubtlessly the head of the biologists since the other two (Kid and long-haired Gompertz) stood deferentially at his side.

"Good afternoon," he said.

In order to communicate his cheerfulness to us (I believe that in this he had gotten together with Atman), he praised trees, which, in his words, start from the tiniest seeds and in no time at all broaden out, growing rapidly in the shapeless air and filling it with an exhilarating burst of flowers and buds.

And Atman, to make us more disposed to hear him, had honey and immortal lotus blossoms distributed to us.

Nergal, taking advantage of our silence, said that bark changes from tree to tree, and in any tree appears now in one form, now in another, according to the increase or decrease of solar storms. All one had to do, for example, is examine the bark of a fig tree to notice how smooth and tumid it is in May and how it ages and hardens in winter.

(The lotus blossoms were good. Many of the men ate them.)

But what's important, he continued, is the subcortical ring, which contains small canals and nerves around the naked pith. The small square plates, which are fissured with the passage of years and form different sorts of crusts, nourish spider larvae enveloped in tufts, and in a superb fashion they are overrun with worms and ants seeking nourishment and infinitely small trickles of corruptible humors. In turn they are infiltrated by tiny moss and mycelia roots, which make little use of stellar rays and the fertilizing pollen that vigorously travels in air currents.

For Nergal all this was a way of explaining to us in simple terms what develops prodigiously under those scales, it being after all the premonition of the impatient union that every tree expects with its vibrating elements. This is indirectly demonstrated by butterflies which, to potentiate the bitter-tasting bark (which is eagerly open to the animal kingdom), go die within it and transform themselves, as the days go by, into flowering grains and leaves.

"Hey," cried Nergal, "why hesitate to be the first to take the step toward that which every tree has been yearning to achieve for centuries?"

Luckily, Mansur was far away and continued to speak with the crabs that slowly traveled beside him, and with the stones that the river current succeeded in turning over laboriously.

Yahin was sniffing the scent of a lotus blossom.

Only Pino remained unconvinced. He looked at Nergal pensively but kept silent so as not to render an action we had considered very simple, more difficult.

He said: "So be it. But ours is becoming a voyage into the unthinkable, a game of linking unconnected ideas and of death. Aren't we going to be knocking our heads against a brick wall?"

Drop-of-blood laughed scornfully, pointing out that we would repeat ourselves indefinitely in a trajectory suspended between the past and the future. That was a big mistake because it was like curling up in a closed roll without exits.

"Come on," interrupted Atman. "Do we or do we not want to focus on the unresolved question of the thanatobird?"

No one objected, nor did Mansur have a desire to do so, believing that his word could come up from the lowest creatures in a direct path to all of us.

All night long we spoke of this union of a human substance with a vegetal one. And no one paid attention to Diofar, whom Al-Hakim, who had returned for this very purpose, brought into the hut.

One of the most controversial issues was the tree to be chosen for the graft. Besides biological criteria, which were foreign to us, there were also the feelings, personal tastes, attitudes of the group and even the divine qualities that some wanted to attribute to the vegetal entity.

Some proposed an olive because it is not very sensitive to the meteorology of the seasons and could, therefore, protect the animal-vegetal concrescence; others proposed an almond, which blossoms unfailingly in February and in March, exactly the period we were in; and still others opted for a hawthorn, whose spiny structure could protect the new being from birds as well as from beetles.

Then Rowley, following his strange and illogical ideas, spoke of a man-wood creature which, expanding and growing, molecule by molecule, could encompass the immutable instants and origins of an infinite space-time.

Abdfilip advised using a common oak or a thick turkey oak, similar to each other in that they produce acorns and are covered with many fronds under which it is easy to start a fire without it catching on the bark, and likewise to rekindle that fire if it should go out.

Pino, seeing that his silent opposition was useless, begged us to choose a lemon tree, a cedar or a tree still more pleasant such as a rose tree, from which the soul could evaporate subtly in the scent of the budding flowers.

Who knows how we managed to agree on a carob, a Mediterranean tree, as Atman explained, that could hide the graft from outsiders. What is more, it is an evergreen with tough small and large leaves, and with very small purplish flowers that blossom in the autumn. And that was not all. Its pods contain seeds that are reddish and very hard, and that were once used for weighing gold and precious stones. Moreover, its red-veined bark would protect the new being from bad weather and give it nourishment thanks to the great circulation with which it is endowed.

Instinctively we all turned our eyes to the carob that, growing in the middle of the large crag opposite Qalat-Minaw, stretched out its branches over the Wadi Hamm, licking the surface of the water with the tips of its longer branches.

"I believe it's the most suitable tree," said Nergal, stroking its leaves.

He and his followers wanted to start the work immediately, but Al-Hakim (and many others shared his view) advised waiting for the hour that falls between twilight and evening. According to him, that is the time when bodily fluxes intensify, and everyone is aware of his nonbeing. That is also the time when a sense of a void and a lack of meaning arises in all things perhaps because of the light from the west, which becomes less intense and slowly grazes the earth. It is then that whoever for years has dreamed of finding the truest island of them all in some desolate region feels the void-death sentence more.

Nergal smiled, and Atman unexpectedly said that the corpuscular essence of the sunset could diminish visible emotions and thus help the graft.

That is why we waited for the last solar rays to strike the top of the carob with a red-violet halo.

A central branch was chosen, a real shoot hidden in the mass of leaves. The work was begun there.

I could describe it in all its complexity, but I do not think it worthwhile to mention the slowness or swiftness of each act and each procedure.

Al-Hakim had brought little Diofar, who was wrapped in his veils and was profoundly asleep from the soporific scents he had inhaled. No one recognized the child nor suspected (except those who had debated the matter) that it was Aramea's son. Unaware of the men's intentions, she had been brought to the town through some ruse and along country roads that had clouded her thoughts.

(I suppose Nergal, Kid and Gompertz grafted the child to the vascular tissue of the branches by his pedial, humeral and temporal arteries.) Evening was not long in coming, so we worked with torches, but soon, because of the inclination of the sky and the ensuing opposition of the air, the almost full moon arose and brought about changes in the countryside and in the men's hearts, predisposing them to sadness and dissolving their passions of thought and love. This, I believe, was the principal factor that dispelled and allayed the fear of the experiment, extending the feelings of everyone (even the most humble representatives of Pino's squad) in an oscillating and vacuous future in which the yellow clouds, the constellation of Leo, the bushes, the mantises and the men were inserted into a circuit of indifferent existence.

We had scattered all around, some sitting on rocks, others reclining on their side and still others feeling very sad—all dimly lit by distant, widespread flashes of lightning that interlaced with emanations of the earth and the firmament.

Inside the carob, the work continued on the invisible joints and the delicate fibers of peduncles and leaves of an obscure substance.

Then, Atman, pointing to a snail climbing up the stalk of a thistle, whispered to me that this mixture of man and tree could signify not the end but the beginning of reverse grafts to be effected on small trees, on bushes and on specimens of swaying grass.

"And that's not all," he exclaimed, placing a finger on the snail, which for a second retreated into its shell. Once a connecting ring was obtained between "big" and "small," we could transport human essence step by step in an incandescent, self-renewing magma toward soft concretions of clay, and ultimately into a thick rocky mass. Passing thus from thought to vegetal essence, and from green molecules united in gelatinous complexes with detractions and connections to atomic aggregates, that is, to a granular jumble of material and void, we could perhaps find causes and principles that would allow us to calmly reconstruct our lost past in a universe that we could freely control in its series of oscillations.

Atman, contrary to his usual demeanor, became excited and continued to speak to me of symbols and models, while in his eyes the slow-moving moon gave our territory another appearance.

A few of the men had fallen asleep next to the trunks of a few poplars, while the majority followed the minute incisions in the bark and the flesh. It was not a common operation, since a genetic material had to be duplicated, transmuting the equilibrium of two different natures without sudden breaks.

When Uncle Pino approached us, Atman, perhaps not to worry him further, remained silent.

That night, we could not even hear the birds. As the moonshine gradually diminished, the expanding constellations were more clearly visible above us in the middle of an unusual length of spaces.

We spent the entire night waiting.

When the sky turned pale because of the imminent dawn made brighter by the north wind, I spotted the grafted branch, and I did not clearly understand to what extent the leaves, nightly dew, medicinal essences, indescribable scents and tiny swollen parts of Diofar formed part of an integrated whole. The branches rose slowly or retreated, bending down with a vermicular motion possibly caused by the slight breeze or the new life seething within them.

Nergal, despite his fatigue, was satisfied. He said that the modalities of existence could indeed be conceived in infinite systems, without at same time interfering with memory, death or love.

He advised sheltering the branch on which Diofar had been grafted. Finally, we all agreed that, to counterbalance one another emotionally, a melancholic and a phlegmatic should guard the carob and thus protect the new human inflorescence from possible corruption.

VI

During those days other men had joined us from the various encampments to help us with the many tasks needed in the valley to broaden and improve our exploration.

Leaving the bottom of the valley, we hiked up a small road toward the high ground of Qamut, which could be spotted amid its stone towers and green hedges.

It was improbable that the showers would return, since wispy clouds dissipated in sleepy spirals like smoke in the sky. We were still vaguely distressed over the past events concerning the graft, but thank goodness, as we proceeded, a sense of liberation came upon us because the rocks that rose up all around us, and whose small gullies and potholes hid blooming yellow camomiles, rare asphodels and fragrant calamints, were not very high.

Abdfilip, at the head of the group, spoke incessantly. He said he was convinced that our mission would be accomplished in Qamut. Nevertheless, he pointed to some rocks, extolling the beauty of their crystalline or chalky structures. He also indicated veins in some ridges containing emeralds and rubies that shone because of the brightness of the already risen sun, and that, according to him, our guide, were immortal because of their immobility.

Obviously, these were observations that rendered the tortuous road merry and indirectly gave us a chance to gaze at the terraces below, which were exposed to the increasing light of the day.

Atman had returned to his calculations before dawn.

Bethsam advised us to have breakfast before confronting the new tasks. He told us to sit on a plateau that was bounded by two tall cypresses and some olive trees. There was no lack of provisions. The earth fumed slightly because it was still sopping wet, and it already portended our desire for very shady woods.

"Hey now," said Yahin. "Why don't we sing?"

Because of unresolved fears, not everyone felt like doing so, but gradually a few intoned some rustic love songs and short madrigals reechoed a thousand times by the still darkened gorges and the multitude of flourishing grasses. But they immediately stopped singing because their altered voices betrayed their hesitation and, I believe, a tacit regret for what was coming between us and the "flying force."

Then Al-Hakim, following the rhythm of our breakfast, very, very softly intoned an Arabic dirge, which we perceived as being a sweet mixture of tunes. It was neither high nor low, but radiated uniformly from all things which to our sleepy eyes seemed to run away and disappear in deceptive circles.

Many of the men finished only half of the meal—black olives, honey, walnuts, biscuits, ricotta, almonds (all spread out on the ground)—and rested their heads against the trunks of small trees, on a myrtle or directly on the clods.

"Just look at them!" murmured Yahin. "They're sleeping." Al-Hakim sang, and sleep overtook several of our other companions, dimming their eyes and minds. A few crows flew overhead. I too felt myself becoming sluggish and starting to totter because of that sound, and the lights and birds that filled the valley. It seemed to me that Al-Hakim was not alone, but was surrounded by other singers who accompanied him in certain vocal passages. The rising chant reverberated from crag to crag in the silence of the entirely deserted countryside, toward the Wadi Hamm, where dark things lit up and everything glowed clearly under the newly risen sun. Uncle Pino, blinking his eyes, said that we were resting too long, but he could not get up. With awkward movements of his fingers, he tried to remove the concentration of sleep and colors from his eyes. The only one who managed to do anything was Rowley. As he ate, he marked unequal numbers and a series of geometric figures on the damp soil. It was a short rest because, when the dirge slowly came to an end, Al-Hakim interrupted our sleep. Shaking a small bunch of wormwood twigs, he said: "What are you doing? Sleeping?"

"Let's go!" shouted Pino.

But Yahin wanted first to offer us some wine from an old carafe; it was like water animated by a little rosy devil that stung the palate and made ideas reemerge.

The ascent continued. We saw two butterflies (the first of the season) flying off some windflowers that were almost black and had twisted stems. Someone collected a few flint chips that smoked in a rivulet of stones suddenly cascading from some clay, and finally Abdfilip, Rowley and Bethsam were attracted by a small field of licorice plants from which they pulled off the roots to suck on. Before long, we would enter the path leading to Le Portelle, which appeared in a split rock. We stopped frequently because we were looking for the tiniest mysterious particles, the effects of the sun on the stones, dark, rising currents of air circulating under us in bramble-covered depressions. But the area, abounding in unusual trees, such as young pistachios, distracted many of our companions from the tasks we had planned to undertake. Moreover, we could hear a confused ringing that reached us from the farthest windward crags, moving away and repeating itself behind the marvelous backdrop of olive trees.

"Hmm, what's that?" wondered Yahin. "Shepherds?"

Mansur noted unforeseen relationships in the various heaps of clods, in the sun's movements or in a few birds that he saw fly toward our left in sparse flashes of fleeting shadows. Rowley grew angry and said that the directions in which the birds flew were of no interest to our exploration. And Mansur said (and in this he was in agreement with Abdfilip) that things could escape the vigilance of the group up there in Qamut, which for years was an inviolate heath because the peasants had emigrated elsewhere.

We went on. The sandy rock of Le Portelle attracted a countless number of solar vapors. Dusk, which was already almost upon us after our slow and uncertain ascent, opened up in an immense circle of red-hot, smoky air.

"Hey, what's happening?" said Pino suddenly.

The carob tree, to the right of whoever is arriving, seemed to be escaping its ancient shapes as if it had grown excessively from the streams of light crenalating the tips of its highest branches with

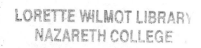

very red dots. Scent-laden herbs sprouted in the gorges and on the rocky elevations.

"Oh, everything has changed!" observed Bethsam. "It's been years since I've come up here."

We went to the left between banks of sandstone that stood out clearly on both sides of the path. Some of these banks were surrounded by reddish flowers; others were very white because of the asphodels that had bloomed among the emerging strips of bulbs. We passed by Syssant's abandoned house, with its roof covered with pellitory, and found ourselves on the plain of Qamut, near the Siculian necropolis, whose dark grottos were immersed in sparse, amorphous vegetation, with little closed snails adhering to the stalks of thistles and to rocks.

The ringing became distant, and was perceptible only if we remained still and listened. Yahin, who always noticed even the smallest things, cried out:

"Oh, for heaven's sake, why?"

We looked at where he was pointing and saw some rivulets descending from a rocky summit; it was not water but milk that, foaming slightly, was gradually scattering amid the closed snails.

"Where are we?" asked Pino.

If you looked carefully, you could see on the ground a great number of hoofprints made by sheep and goats. So Abdfilip explained to us that the shepherds who passed through those heights were unable to curdle the milk because the towns to be reached were far away, and had, therefore, milked the animals and allowed much of that food to go to waste.

Rowley laughed and, dipping his finger into the liquid, tasted it and said,

"It's good."

Looking at the ruins of a house and those of a church with only one arch still standing, we saw Ziritia, Muslim, Mariela and Gheorghy amid clumps of chicory and hazelnut trees.

"Hey, where are you going?" they shouted.

And Uncle Pino retorted, "Do we always have to run into you?"

They drank peacefully at a small cascade of milk that, falling, dispersed in a thousand trickles from a small hill of stones. Ziritia, hiding then emerging from the clump of hazelnut trees, was carrying some hives from which she was squeezing out the honey. The children were going over to the fountains of milk and, immediately after, to the honeycombs.

"What a fine surprise!" observed Kid, having followed us on Nergal's advice to study the composition of the flora of that high ground.

He first stooped to drink the milk, wetting his little beard, which turned silver on his chin. Abdfilip advised not letting that food dry nor allowing it to be absorbed by the thistle roots and the stunted little plants. I tasted the honey. It was sweet. The five children were going back and forth, and they were laughing, saying that only they knew that town and those places, which were now uninhabited.

The majority of Pino's men were joking as if a weight had been taken off their minds. They drank milk and honey from their cupped hands, and, not satisfied, went to find hives on which, luckily, few bees had returned from their peregrinations. Seeing this, Pino grumbled,

"Are you losing your wits?"

But nobody paid any attention to him; they continued to sip milk and honey, or honeymilk that, I believe, dulled the mind a bit.

The unexpected scene had sidetracked us. From the opposite side, in the plateaus, thick, uncultivated clumps of wheat, barley and oats stood out amid stones encrusted with fragments of shells upon which luminescent gases of the sunset evaporated.

I too drank from a spout of milk rendered tastier by the thyme over which it had passed, and Lucrezio offered me a honeycomb split in two, its small cells quite full of honeyed mush. The only one who did not follow our example was Yahin, who spoke to us of the fertility of that abandoned zone, where rows of early broad beans, fig trees, mulberry bushes and purple apricot trees had made it rosy and green for the wayfarer who might reach it from the four corners of the earth. There were no rocks piled up in dead, grassless glades, as there are now, or, on the contrary, an uncontrolled lush growth of thistles and brambles forming large, impervious islands in the thresholds of the farmhouses and in the passes of the crags.

But no one listened to him since we were absorbed in the white flow whose tiny canals, foamy wisps and bubbles broke the monotony of the limestone hill and invited the few crows high above to stop in midair to observe the white design in the desert of stones.

Satisfied and stuffed, we sat down, facing the west. We could not follow the line of the horizon because of the solar vortex that from the bottom of its abyss obscured our vision. Lucrezio and Bethsam hid behind some arid prickly pears whose thick leaves reverberated an extraordinary number of dense fluxes.

"Oh what a nuisance!" said Rowley, accustomed as he was to towns built on misty promontories.

And then, perhaps because we were half-drunk from the milk and honey which still furred our palates and hearts, Lucrezio, leaning out from the clump of prickly pears, said to us: "Don't you see?"

"What?" asked Abdfilip, as he collected the last spurts of milk from the sand quarry in a jug.

"The suns!"

"What are you trying to say?" asked Pino, who, tired, passed the time spreading honey on a cluster of snails that were motionless on the twigs of a hedge.

It was not easy to turn our gaze toward the horizon, on which masses of air navigated and spread progressively downward over crags, caves and woods.

"Two suns!" shouted Lucrezio. "Could I be cross-eyed?"

It was necessary to shield the sun with our hands to better make out those two spheres whose turbulent red masses lit up the western mountains, which changed appearances in the last movement of the day.

According to Yahin, we had become dimwitted, because if we examined the western mountains carefully, we would not find anything unusual. In fact, he said, all we had to do is shut an eye to notice that the sun was one as always, that one eye sees as much as two and perhaps more if swiftly rotated within its socket. He concluded that we were crazy to pursue the arcane and to confuse it with what happened every day and at every instant; it was time to return to our usual occupations and not to create so easily fantasms of men, of fish nourished by the wave, of birds and even those of deities with supreme attributes.

The very bright light struck all of us, including the children, who watched from atop a boundary wall, with the tawny leaves of fig and honeyberry trees above their heads.

Rowley, belching milk vapors, said that even by looking through a fig leaf one could make out two solar masses close to one another and rotating, one within the other. According to him, it was not a question of accidental qualities of the Qamutan atmosphere, but probably that of a predetermined phenomenon (linked to the spring equinox) which caused an intensification of waves in extraterrestrial circles and a disturbance in the timing of planetary orbits.

Several, still sucking honeycombs, said that it was not important whether one sun or two or three, illuminating the array of fixed stars from top to bottom, descended in outer space. Sleep, honey and milk soothe sentiments and do not affect either the rising or setting of the sun and the moon, nor the meridians encircling the terraqueous globe; rather, it was the sound of distant sheepbells and armfuls of thyme and calamints, from which scents emanated very strongly in every direction, eastward as well as westward.

Fortunately, the sunset ended with millions of scattered beams and a darkening of colors, although many of the summits that stood out from the rest of the heaths and valleys rose up like peaks pierced with purple.

A great many of our companions slept, belching sweetish vapors. I saw Muslim, followed by Ziritia, Emanuele, Mariela and Gheorghy, run on the sand toward the grottos, and then on the uneven glade. With the top of their heads, the top of their shoulders and their darting legs lit up by the remaining light of the sun, they went in and out of those hiding places, one right after the other. They looked red, then yellow, depending on how the sun's light struck them, until, going from burrow to burrow, they disappeared in the shadows of that very ancient necropolis.

VII

Before news of Aramea reached us, we pitched camp above Gianforte, on a plateau sheltered from the cool night air.

Below us there was a deep valley where day after day (as, however, was the case in all other areas) plants and flowers covered the eroded masses, the entrances to the caves, and the pebbly shores of springs whose waters descended in thousands of rivulets, making the areas we crossed glisten.

The few peasants still scattered throughout the lands of Qalat-Minaw, learning of our arrival and the strange things we were looking for in the fields and valleys, hid in haylofts, secluded dens and even in large hollows of oak and olive trees. And in the seeming inertia of those days, we noticed that they warned one another with preestablished signals in an effort to prevent us from bringing them chaos and ruin.

One late afternoon, Abdfilip, pointing to a spot near Qaltag, said to us,

"Do you see that black thing?"

"Which one?" replied Rowley, who, looking up, was mentally conducting some celestial observations.

"I mean down there! Down there."

It was a plume of smoke ascending in slow, dark circles that kept changing their shapes—but not so much because of the wind, since everything was clear and still—and dividing into several equal parts, broadening, or contracting into a dark narrow streak. A little later, other plumes coming out of invisible hollows arose from the heights and, forming successive spirals, dissipated in the thin air.

Very quickly we realized that we were dealing with a prearranged, secret language. Uncle Pino grew angry because of this, seeing himself spied upon by the peasants, who were afraid we would discover the degrees and orbits of the fireball's route.

There was, in fact, a correspondence between those plumes of smoke and what we were thinking and planning in our daily work, which consisted in the formulation of hypotheses and various justifications for our ideas.

Often the peasants anticipated us, learning from the shepherds and the vagabonds, who were purposely beating on the trunks of olive trees, what in Qalat-Minaw even Atman and Albumasar, the head of the scholars, imagined in their hopeful dreams to have attained.

And so, a new element was added to the episode regarding Aramea and Diofar, something, however, that Salvat had already foreseen: the lack of due consideration for the effluences that might be emanating from the body of our father.

Pino, in his astonishment, asked,

"What are we trying to get to?"

Yahin answered,

"It's an endless course. Why don't we give it all up?"

Rowley and Kid smiled, the former saying that if we did so, we would be outside the continuity of matter, and could neither know or find out at which hypothetical levels the rhythmical or continual oscillations were occurring between the remains of Donnané, our father, and the walls of the house, or even beyond them, in an impalpable and incorporeal void. Mansur contradicted Rowley, maintaining that such effluences could perpetually disturb or purify the rivers, springs, woods and clouds as the hours and seasons changed.

In short, our rushing from one extreme point of the territories of Qalat-Minaw to another, and our radial exploration of its familiar features, suddenly projected us from the existence to the non-existence of our lost origins.

Then Kid, ceasing to run his hand over the woody bark of a tree uprooted by some solitary peasant, spoke. He said that if we would turn our attention away from the vegetal universe that amid a cluster of leaves and arabesque fronds and in a stream of images brought us into its subterranean and airy matrix, we would make the *vexata quaestio* more muddled. What could we gather from our deceased father? Whispers? Waves? Imperceptible sounds? Rowley, stretching out his arms, objected that, at that point, nothing could escape from a body from which every conceivable opening for sound, whirlpools and solar whirlwinds was excluded. He said that that body was trapped in an interminable lethargy which would soon dissolve it within the gloomy meanders of the earth, where it would be wrapped above and around by the rising of lunar veils, waves and damp clods in which grasses grew. Our deductions and hypotheses only hindered the search for the inexistent substance, for that overflow of love which had become frozen forever.

Toward evening Atman and Nergal joined us so that we might analyze the insoluble unknowns and formulate a plan that would bind Aramea to languishing dreams and to the flapping wings of the great many birds that spring had brought.

It was an unusual evening owing in part to the presence of Al-Hakim. He was tired of the uncertain outcome of Diofar's graft, and even though he did not express his doubt to us (which was greatly increased by Aunt Agrippa in Qalat-Minaw, where he had spent a day), he was convinced that Aramea was an insurmountable obstacle to the entire operation because of certain vapors escaping from her body. He had, therefore, decided to make her less homogeneous, that is, to make her human substance heterogeneous.

In short, we were at a crossroads since, as we learned indirectly, Aunt Agrippa, Al-Hakim and Lucrezio opposed our ideas.

But we paid little attention to Al-Hakim since we were intent on examining closely whether something of our father had remained and could still be captured.

Atman, for his part, maintained that the relationship existing between the thanatobird and the semblances of our father was of capital importance, considering the fact that the above-mentioned emanations could constitute quantities of waves definable as a series of shocks that pass out of the body and lose themselves in a frenzied multiplicity, or unity, of centrifugal orbits.

He suspected that we were at the threshold of an immense universe, and that we would perhaps get lost in subterranean passages and in the investigation of laws and principles that could assume the appearance of incontrovertible truths.

And to relax we strolled in groups of two or three down a path, among herbs and stones, free, in this manner, to pursue our nascent hypotheses.

However, according to Rowley, Nergal, Atman and Salvat (whose personal opinions about the matter differed slightly), we should record the last events of our father's mind so as not to leave anything obscure in this entire affair. According to them, even though these things were mortal, they could not have been suddenly extinguished within the original being, but alternating with magnetic phenomena and the larvae of sentiments, had to gradually leave the inertia of the body to dissipate in perpetual shadows that multiplied ad infinitum.

Pino, breaking off an olive branch and scattering the leaves all around, said that we would uselessly lose time and defile the memory of his brother if we sought insignificant clues of the arithmetical fluidity of dead particles and seeds of thought. Were the little leaves he scattered around still the branch of an olive tree? Why reduce the thinking remains of his brother, granted they existed, to graphs and numbers, since very great toils and extreme hardships no longer exist in death's void? At the most, there is an irradiation of imponderable fluxes which, though very small, thin and fast, imbue the surrounding regions with a transitory mobility similar to the soul.

And one evening, Al-Hakim, seated on the ground in our tent, looked at us askance and said that Aunt Agrippa, to whom none of us would give a hearing, even though she was shrewder than any of us, had the ability to run her hand along the body of a dead person and feel the slightest variations of life and thought that still existed. Moreover, if she so desired, she could evoke them with the scents of incense, camphor, aloe and gray amber. And that's not all, because she could also distinguish the etheric soul from the fluidic one. The latter was easily perceptible because of the sensiferous impulses it caused, and the former was vaguely distinguishable as it emanated from the limbs in vibrant filaments and in small, rapid whirlwinds that, doubling, moaning, choking and reemerging, scatter lovingly on the currents of rivers, on the ocean, in flourishing buds and in the lunar halo.

"Now, what are you saying?" objected Nergal, opening the tent to make us see the nocturnal landscape.

Then Al-Hakim spoke to us with a gentle, persuasive voice of the possibility of evoking, if we wished, the red dragon, Athal, Bathel, Nothe, Jhoram, Gabellyn and Semenej. But Bethsam cut in, saying that it was time to put an end to hollow words, senseless suppositions and empty formulas. Pointing to the campsite, where the lights shone in a phosphorescent cluster, and farther on to the mountain of lights of Qalat-Minaw, and still farther on to those of Qaltag, which proceeded upward like a flock of sheep, and to those too of Grammichele overshadowed by the haze of the heights and by the crown of woods, with downcast eyes he whispered as if to himself,

"There was Gesumino Bethsam, and now he is no longer;
there was Salvatore Bethsam, and now he is no longer;
there was Donnanè, and now he is no longer;
there was Grandmother Cecè, and now she is no longer;
there was Grandfather Giuseppe, and now he is no longer;
there was Uncle Casaccio, and now he is no longer;
there was Aunt Pina, and now she is no longer;
there was farmer Filippo, and now he is no longer;
there was Bino Giordano, and now he is no longer;
there was Pippo Calì, and now he is no longer;
there was farmer Angelo, and now he is no longer."

It was a tired and trembling voice. Except for Rowley, Nergal and Kid, who silently went outside to look at the soon-to-be-extinguished lights of the towns, no one spoke at that moment, and Al-Hakim, as well, stood with bowed head, perhaps searching his memory repeatedly for past names, deeds and places, each with its own sign of the zodiac, in a whirling path of celestial trails.

Not much later, Atman and I also went out to the clearing, which was slowly being drenched with heavy dew. Going down the path, we met Rowley, Nergal and Kid, who, leaning against an oak tree, were smoking in silence. There, in a whisper, not to disturb our sleeping companions, under the darting bats, we decided to extend our love peregrination elsewhere, to a larger area, because certainly our father had been a center of sentiment-heart, of messages conceived deep down which, in the shadows of night and in those of day, had spread from him to other men and to us, his children and relatives. And now that he was following the fatal fall with preestablished regularity, we had to feel close to him, deriving those remnants of thought presumably gushing forth from his body after his death.

VIII

We were forced to stay a few more days on the plateau of Qamut. While Atman and Nergal were returning to town, we unexpectedly saw Abel, the visitor, arrive. He was wrapped in a black cape.

"Oh, it's you!" he shouted. "Where have you been hiding out?"

"What have you come here for?" Pino asked.

Abel took off his cape and said that he was exhausted because he had climbed the rocky road against the wind. Then, sitting down on the trunk of a felled tree, and wiping his sweat with a large, red-trimmed handkerchief, he informed us that when Aramea awoke from her long, induced sleep, she asked about Diofar and was not satisfied with the assurances of those present who told her how happily her baby had spent his days in the sun, amid the haystacks and the holm oaks. He added that, soon, when no longer watched, she would run off toward the Wadi Hamm. Each of us thought of Nergal, who, shortly before, in waving goodbye to us with a lit cigar held between his fingers, had assured us that Aramea's fate would not be of any concern to us, nor would it incite the ignorant populace of Qalat-Minaw to take reprisals against us or to entertain unvoiced suspicions in the streets or on the doorsteps of their houses should they learn of the graft. Unfortunately, the graft, among other things, was not going well because of the lack of hemolymph and the disharmony among the cellular fires, which did not succeed in permeating one another through the small canals and mucilaginous mixtures. But there was nothing to worry about, Nergal continued, because all he needed was one dark night to think it over seriously, and the outcome of the graft would be resolved favorably.

I believe that Nergal and Aunt Agrippa shared the same secret goals, even if they followed divergent paths of reasoning, such as we thought we had at first understood.

However, during those days, without us noticing anything, Abel, Al-Hakim and Lucrezio, rising at dawn, resorted to the indirect help of Bethsam. The latter, still believing that one could surely find the fireball under the guise of a bird, would post himself on the surrounding heights or in the grassy lowlands. He went there to listen to the birds sing, to identify the different species, to track them if possible and finaily to shoot the ones he felt had unusual flight patterns or calls.

While the three men followed him, they looked for shoots, early spikes and flowers with particular orientations. They distinguished one from the other by means of their essential combinations of scents, and finally hid them in safe shelters.

Before separating Aramea's body from her soul, Aunt Agrippa decided to put her into a spell, the sort that extremely rare arboreal fragrances put people in when they are applied with occult powers.

Lucrezio happened to tell us this, one evening, when he was tipsy from having drunk too much wine. Even though he spoke enigmatically, he gave us clearly to understand that for Aunt Agrippa, for Al-Hakim, for himself and for so many others (who were deceiving us), it was in the corollas, pollen and very thin fibers of the gynoecium that fragrant emanations were arising, and that contained, in a mixture of elements, heat, the imperceptible sounds of beetles, lunar filtrations and the extreme lightness of bird flights.

Rowley, Kid and my brother, Salvat, wasted a lot of time with their calculations and diagrams from which they were to determine ihe routes probably taken by the bird. Nevertheless, all of us together ordered Abdfilip to follow the three friends who were looking for those vegetal components throughout the lands that had been ideally divided into equal parts. They often followed in the footsteps of Bethsam, who, the thinker that he was, wanted to convert the vibrant currents of air suddenly traversed by birds into visible numbers and signs.

While we spent our days wasting time, being unable to establish a rational hierarchy of the phenomena that had appeared, Al-Hakim continued searching throughout the steep lands of Gianforte and down amid the alfalfa fields of the deep valleys, which were usually deserted and covered with frost that glistened very brightly under the early sun. He would even go out at midnight followed by Lucrezio, because he was looking for the proper astral moments to cut the stems of the so-called sad flowers, which intensified their emanations only in the dark but were perceptible when the wind blew.

We learned from Abdfilip that besides rare holly, which could be found in the hidden recesses of the valley, and spiny asparagus, they collected bloodroot, heliotrope, heather, acanthus, vervain, olive buds, henbane, iris, roots of newly sprouted broad bean plants, poppy in the bud, ferns and moss. At first they scraped the soft, hairy surfaces with silver knives, and mostly the parts facing north, where the sun's rays are less strong. And finally, they selected leaves and petals of the meadow geranium.

In their tent they arranged them in small sacks of linen and hemp; and when the moon waned, they exposed them to the rays that, because of the thin crescent moon, were concentrated on the tops of olive trees, in ditches, on torrents and on swampy, submerged vegetation, with countless lights and almost imperceptible shadows.

This happened in the period that goes from the twenty-third to the twenty-ninth day of the lunar cycle. Uncle Pino advised not resorting to disgusting operations such as these, which made a mockery of our fatiguing travels through valleys and over mountains.

But Atman and the scholars, notified of this, did not object. They said that it was necessary to give our group, which was besieged by so many uncommon facts, the possibility of unleashing its imagination in some delightful game; but in reality they were pursuing an idea useful to their goal.

We soon learned that on a moonless night, when dogs were barking in the mountainous deserts of Qaltag and, even closer, on the roundish slopes of Qamut and in the invisible rock heaps that along the roads marked the curves of the fields and those of the sunken plains below, Al-Hakim, Lucrezio and Abel returned to Qalat-Minaw with their strongly-scented leaves, roots and seeds. The only one to notice them was Rowley, but he did not fully realize the importance of the three men's departure since he was absorbed in observing very limpid streams of stars that sparkled toward the east in exaggerated inclinations.

I cannot tell you in detail what happened during those days in Qalat-Minaw since the news leaking out was uncertain and unclear, and we were obliged to look for traces of the thanatobird in the blackthorn thickets of the crag of Gianforte, despite the fact that Abdfilip continued repeating to us, "What are we doing? Trying to ward off some bad luck up here? Let's go back to town."

I can only tell you that for a few days after she experienced her first sudden fears over the fate of her son, Aramea calmed down when they told her that she had best not go to the Wadi Hamm since it was infested with hornets and swarms of wasps. But her calm was short-lived. One night, she ran off, heading for the torrent, but Al-Hakim had cast a spell on her with perfumes made from dense herbal sediments. And to calm her down, he brought her a tulle veil in which her son had been wrapped, and she, smelling it, said that it was impregnated with milk, black earth, the scents of rustling palm trees, and Diofar's little heart. She became silent and absorbed in thought. Being surrounded on all sides by subtle, penetrating fragrances that, assailing her, were sometimes bewitching and long-lasting, she felt lighter, as if she were hovering in a new human substance. And in order to linger longer in those scents, she secretly smeared herbal creams on her black eyebrows, on the lower part of her abdomen and on her hips. Meanwhile, the gloomy mood saddening her eyes and forehead deepened, so that she no longer loved the blueness of dawn, the sparkles of Qalat-Minaw's one thousand roofs and the views of the remote mountain passes.

She began to think less about Diofar. In the evening, as she reached the heights of the Castle, she looked at the slow closing of the mallow, white rose and umbel leaves, which were heavy because of the sunset's very long rays, and she privately rubbed her white arms in those plants; or, worse, as the days passed, she sat alone on a rock and waited for the bell towers to announce the arrival of evening, dissipating the joyful radiance left by the sun on the mountain ridges and in the rocky gullies of the cliffs. She seemed less and less disposed to accept the monotony of life.

Aunt Agrippa secretly watched her as she underwent changes brought on by the scents of the flowers. To make her draw closer to the infinitesimal and unexpressed sentiments of minerals, she sent Abel to her with small pieces of coral mixed with malachite, emeralds and lapis lazuli, having him say to her,

"Come on, have some fun with these precious stones."

Aunt Agrippa waited for signs that would assure her that the young women's nature had become bicorporeal, airy and damp, as well as molecular and hot, before resorting to her arts, which freed one from the fear of being bound to what is thin, to what is empty, to terrestrial accelerations and to the contagion of vegetal putrefaction.

One day at dusk, Aramea, sitting on the sandstone ridge of Salinardo amid clumps of thyme, and looking at the smoke coming from some old gates, saw a blackcap flying high above. Attracted by the bird, she followed it down the twisted path leading to the Wadi Hamm and, through a series of detours, left behind Qalat-Minaw (which grew red within wandering clouds) and arrived at the torrent.

"Where are you going, beautiful woman?" a peasant returning with his donkey asked her.

Aramea did not answer but pointed to the forgotten holm oak, which in the shifting of the last light of the day absorbed the flaming rays of the setting sun from above and the grayness of the wrinkled clay and the river current from below.

Then she vividly remembered Diofar and, washing her face and hands in a pond, she quietly climbed the tree through its most protruding branches, keeping to the right. Thinking she might find her son up there, she called out to him and listened in the hope of hearing his breathing or an echo of his crying. When she arrived at the top, she spread out a piece of satin cloth that someone had left behind in his haste to steal her child. Gently separating the small branches and buds that jutted out from the bark and flourished there, she continued to look for Diofar or his shadow, which could be mistakenly seen on the crown, but she found nothing but the final blaze of the setting sun. Addressing the sunset, she raised her fingers, rotating and curving them against the rays. She looked down at the clusters of leaves and at the old acorns still attached to the woody matrix by their small dead leaf stalks, spotting nothing there but a tangle of rising shadows. And she looked ever more at the sun, begging it not to set and to bring her at least images of the sandy deserts. But only the solitary gurgling of the river reached her.

She thought that Al-Hakim and our other companions had tricked her, taking her from Diofar and her beloved Yusuf, who was supposed to join her soon. And she felt a desire to rub vegetable pap on her nape, resting her chin, mouth and heart on the boughs of that holm oak so that its fibers and diaphanous sap would tremble within her.

Nor can I relate every detail of the woman's fate, except for the end she met. It seems that during the night she slept on that tree, waiting for a cry or a scent to tell her where her son was, but nothing came to her if not dormice, rabbits and moles that gathered under the holm oak late at night, in the bare open space, to dance and playfully chase after one another. For her, it was not an easy life.

She ran through the mountains and the countryside, her mind closed to everything but Diofar, who, unbeknownst to her, was dying inside the carob. And, leaving along the way scents of blooming flowers and herbs that had sprouted in the ditches and hills, she was almost instinctively followed by some lost sheep, fawns driven out of the forests, orioles, finches and excited chirping sparrows. She did not notice them as she continued along through streams and green recesses. She was certainly out of her mind, or almost so, and she would stop briefly to eat laurel and rosemary leaves, grains of wheat and small blackcap eggs, all the while attracting swarms of gnats that hid her from the shepherds. At night, except for brief, sudden naps, she constantly headed for holm oaks, which she identified from their scent and rustling leaves, and she would climb them to search again and again, finding nothing. Then she would climb down and, breathing in the briny air that reached her from the great expanse of sea, she would go again through sand, mud and the twisting paths of the woods. Lost goats continually followed her, as well as horned owls, hedgehogs, small foxes and moths. There were not three, four or five animals but dozens of them. They sniffed her hands and the hem of her dress, blindly approached her and even plunged into the turbid currents and the marshes. Actually, the rabbits preceded her briskly. But she did not know she was being watched or that her days on earth were numbered, because Atman, Nergal, Pino, Totosimic and our father's other brothers were interested in the foundations on which the semblances of the thanatobird and the deceased whirled, the domination, that is, of the world to which they were ineluctably subject, and which they wanted to seize in the very essence of its spirals.

Al-Hakim followed her from above on a strange mount. It was an eagle that he had tamed on the huge crags of Coste by bringing it skinned snakes, smelly pumpkins, live lambs covered with white poppies, blister beetles and Indian hemp.

The young woman never raised her head since she was absorbed in her wandering, and so the two followed each other in a symmetrical circle of uneven turns, neither she, nor he ever tiring. Al-Hakim flew about on the eagle, that docilely let itself be led toward the east, ever farther and farther toward the east, which swelled in the daytime and, turning in a dizzy spiral of light, dissolved and fell in motionless evenings.

And when Aramea entered the olive woods, occasionally calling Diofar "lamp," "shady palm" and "little bamboo heart," Al-Hakim, fearing she would get lost in the underbrush that he could not see from up there, made the eagle slow down. He felt seized by frenzy, not knowing whether that was the result of the woman's sudden absence or the sun's dazzling rays that scattered in all directions.

Around the young woman everything continued as before, and from the peaks of the Peloritani, from the Dittaino, Gornalunga, Irminio and Salso rivers, from the last patches of snow on the Erei and the Madonie, from the many natural grottos of the island and from the thickets and abysses, birds flew over the path taken by

Aramea, fish darted to and fro in an easterly direction and bees swarmed in the same direction. Some vagabonds thought that if one looked carefully, one would see that some zephyrs which traveled directly from west to east were bending the blossoming pear, peach, laurel and aquatic trees.

This account was related to us by Ibn-al-Atir, a loner who wandered through the countryside and onto the ridges to pick chicory, tying it in bunches with sorghum that grew at the edge of steep cliffs.

Not all of us were inclined to believe him, but our inactivity and the scanty clues of our exploration made us listen to what Ibn-al-Atir gladly blurted out to us between a sip of wine and a mouthful of bread and olives.

Meanwhile, Diofar's graft was doing poorly because of extraneous forces and the lack of symbiosis between human and vegetal particles, mitochondria and chloroplasts, and because of the unrealizable reflux of blood and sap in a single circulation. In brief, the entire operation made us a laughing stock, and of this, Mansur was certain. He told us that we had put the carob and the infant in a state of delirium without achieving the triumph we had expected; on the contrary, we were again proposing to undertake a foul task, as Atman had already informed us through circuitous means, and not only Atman but also Albumasar and the other scholars whom we had never seen, not even in a scattered pattern of shadows. As we rushed from one thing to another, we would inevitably end up losing our sanity in a jumble of inductions and reflections.

But we could not follow Aramea's marked destiny because another question arose in Qalat-Minaw regarding the routes taken by the fireball, and we were therefore forced to retrace our steps and leave our daily investigations to the groups scattered in the above-mentioned lands.

IX

We again met on the heights of the Castle, which overlooked our territories and, beyond them, Etna, whose scarps rose up and seemed to float in the currents and inlets of the Ionian basin.

Atman greeted us with a nod and tried to encourage us (we'll succeed this time!), because he realized how much our uncertainty had deepened.

"And so?" Pino said to him.

Totosimic, Orlando and Geber were strolling under the acacias. Tirtenio had recently arrived from the valley of Pozzillo and, shaking his long black hair, observed that rather than analyzing the practically nothing we had found, we were digressing and losing ourselves in erroneous interpretations.

"This isn't the time for criticism," answered Atman.

He added that the scholars—Albumasar, Eddington, Hubble and Jafar—were advising us to turn our thoughts to the rotating desert of the moon because the great number of messages keeping us chained to a wheel were going there and coming from there.

Uncle Pino scratched his head, and Geber curbed his vexation, grumbling indistinct words. Totosimic wanted to quickly harvest the results of the experiences we would manage to obtain in outer space, whether they be obvious or not. According to him, right after that, we should reverse all of our speculations in the opposite direction. Geber supported his contention.

Some turmoil broke out among us, but it was fortunately quelled by Mansur. He told us that we had misunderstood the five principles of existence, and that, at this point, it was better to continue to turn to the mobile firmament and to the knowledge obtained up above in the millennia of millennia by everything that had emanated from the lands and the seas.

"So be it!" exclaimed Pino, the eldest of the brothers.

And Orlando, supporting him, said,
"Indeed!"

The most enthusiastic of all was Rowley. He said it was senseless to quarrel, now that we were waiting to see our satellite appear and the lights it was sending us on its journey along the endless belt. As he spoke, he was mentally traveling to the stellar sphere.

Peace was restored among us. The only one not participating was Abdfilip, who sat on the rocks of the cliff with some canes in his hand. Bethsam insisted on maintaining the thesis of a real bird to be found in our parts, but in order not to set himself against us for the weak assumptions we were about to use as our guide, he exclaimed,

"Let's go ahead and turn our eyes elsewhere, but even outside the world, I will pursue the birds that inexorably dot the vault of the heavens."

With these words he probably intended to encourage us.

The position of the moon was calculated by using the *National Almanac*, as navigators are wont to do (so, purely by chance, I again found myself at the starting point of the present story), and in order to circumscribe the points occupied during the satellite's year, we applied one thousand and eight hundred corrections to the median longitude of the lunar effluences at dawn, at noon and at the pivotal hour of midnight. In this way, we had a basic picture of what had happened and what could happen through the operations of the thanatobird, which had already left irradiations and traces on the crags tinged with colorful flowers, on the green banks and on the minerals cast into pitch blackness by the night.

It was not an easy task, since we had shifted our ephemeral victories from a terrestrial field to a starry one. We had also done so with the new combinations perceivable in the magnetic lunar fluxes that actually float on the surface of the waters in various directions and in endless waves.

It certainly cannot be said that herbs, marsh waters, slithering or flying animals, rains and winds are present on our earth's satellite. It was necessary, therefore, to take into consideration only earthy or rocky elements and titanium and silica salts, or similar effusive phenomena that make those lands, dissimilar to ours even as to their origins, dark and lucent. There are both obscure areas and tortuous ones, which, in protuberances and crooked lines of false fantasms, shed their soothing light from up there to us in the early flowering of Qalat-Minaw's countryside, and cause all sorts of changes to occur on the surfaces of the waters and on the crowns of the olive trees.

By then we were spending most of our evenings at the Castle, where ivy grew thickly over the ruins. We looked up at the countless variety of sidereal inclinations, or we followed the reflection of the light of stellar domains that traveled in the same direction with a slow, rotating motion. These domains passed over us, going from land to land, over bare rocks and wooded slopes, with a mixture of shadows and bright flickers of light in which we spotted immense forests and distant dead towns.

The days, however, seemed longer than they actually were because all our hypotheses had weakened and because we noted the fallacy in everything.

One afternoon, Atman spread out a large topographic map of our satellite under our eyes so that we could study it. By marking off seas and rocks, we were to become convinced that eventual magnetic bands and black waves of sentiment could reach us from that rocky domain. It was a domain wrapped in heavy bodies spinning for millions of seasons around the pivot of the lunar axis. Yahin, spitting repeatedly, said to us that we had better not lose ourselves in other realms but, instead, seek maidenhair near the springs and small stationary rocks in the torrents.

We ignored him. Drinking wine, rum, spring water or milk, each according to his own preference, and under the guidance of Atman (who claimed that his instructions came from the group of astronomers and scholars), we examined the lunar map, projecting upon it our sentiments, fears and our great desires to leave our suspicions, assumptions, afflictions and unending Hades on that astral body.

Seated in a circle, we repeated the names of oceans and mountain ranges, hills and other topographical features, collecting, perhaps unwittingly, the rarity or density of the moon's lights and effluences.

Atman said, "*Bailly*," and we echoed,
"Bailly"
And further:
"*Mare Humorum*,"
(Mare Humorum);
"*Mare Nubium*,"
(Mare Nubium)
"*Oceanum Procellarum*,"
(Oceanum Procellarum);
"*Mare Imbrium*,"
(Mare Imbrium);
"*Mare Serenitatis*,"
(Mare Serenitatis);
"*Mare Crisium*,"
(Mare Crisium);
"*Mare Tranquillitatis*,"
(Mare Tranquillitatis).

In saying that, we felt less distant from our father and the thanatobird, because we swiftly crossed great stretches of moon and soul. We did so with the simple movement of the changing shadows cast by the new branches of the nearby acacias and lindens.

Every now and then Al-Hakim stopped pursuing Aramea and joined us. Pointing his black beard upward, he smiled, following his ideal flight on vultures, amid lunar spurs. Then, taking advantage of our jeremiads, he had himself transported from those steep rocks into deep valleys where a very strong sun and its shadows reigned, and onto chains of ridges when the satellite became short and very thin. Up there, not even low branchy trees grew, nor those that were smooth and aromatic.

Ever smiling, he told us that on the sides of volcanic rock he used a brush to paint red and blue lines to reproduce the moon's topography. There, long curves stood out, which, after all, were mines of glassy residues where there was no betony, but an abundance of mercury, amethyst and celandine. Then Yahin, with his usual good sense, grumbled, "But what are you saying? What are you saying?"

Al-Hakim, momentarily forgetting the exhausted Aramea, who sat under the face of a mountain, added that the moon, where he saw no trace of our father, was bringing along in its perpetual rotation hoof, balsam, topaz and obon.

Seeing that our meetings on the summit of the town continued far into the night, the few inhabitants of Qalat-Minaw became curious. They climbed up the slope and, hidden among the rocks, watched us without us realizing it.

We made no end of maps, inks, astrolabes (and the divine intellect of love), constantly focusing all our thoughts on the moon, which showed us parts of itself (*Mare Frigoris, Sinus Roris, Mare Nectaris, Mons Heraclitus, Breislak, Dove Lockyer*), with Yahin grumbling ever less, having become sleepy on account of that white face which traveled with its sandy seas and black gullies.

The people of Qalat-Minaw returned. Though skeptical, they cast fear away and showed their eyes and noses to our group, which day after day found itself ever more entangled in the most peculiar conjectures.

Abdfilip, who was always silent, absorbed as he was in making and remaking a flageolet from reeds, noticed that dark scattered crowd. He did not take part in our diatribes but became engrossed in his work, paying no attention, not even to those people.

"Oh, what are you doing?" Uncle Pino once asked him, tired of the glistening lunar light and its white reflections on the mist of the deep valleys.

Abdfilip did not reply. Instead, he showed him not one but two flageolets that he had already diligently prepared.

"I'm talking to you," insisted Pino, and Geber also drew near, making a wry mouth and licking a few tears that had rolled down from his tired eyes.

Abdfilip said that for many years he had looked down at the earth's clods and the morning mist that suddenly glistens, and had not become interested in that miserable strip of earth-mountains that threatens man with a stream that, receding up above, can make drupes wither on the trees, or make them grow endlessly. It is a dark chunk of land that we enjoy calling our satellite, and that we never tire gazing at from our rooftops and from the poplars that rise from the dwarf rivers of Sicily. And absentmindedly he tried a very mellow flageolet, blowing gently and producing some fast and slow sounds that stopped the "slow" advance of our fellow townsfolk.

Uncle Pino was at a loss for words when Abdfilip, perhaps to free himself from his feeling of uneasiness, pointed to the deep valleys below, lost in a lunar curtain. One should seek what remains of our father there, he asserted, and not in the open book of the sky, which has secrets only for fools who feel attracted by its leaden stellar swashing.

That same night, Abdfilip disappeared and did not return the following day, or even the day after. We looked for him along many roads, but, not finding him, we returned to our ascending spiral of doubts.

There was a rumor that Abdfilip was using his flageolets to find the agitated swarms of our father and the whimsical, unpredictable routes taken by the flying demon.

That was probably true because several of our companions and some of the local peasants said that Abdfilip played his instruments in the valleys and woods. Who knows whether he rested, because his musical messages increased in the countryside, especially at dusk.

Moreover, the sounds of his flageolets were not always the same: each day they were different from one moment to the next, depending, among other things, on the solar fluxes and the old man's state of mind, which varied according to how the light and its seeds, and the waves of propitious stars converged on him.

Before long there were many who heard those vibrant airs, those artificial breezes throughout our territories.

Information reached us from the various squads that were camping, but it was sketchy. There were even some who said that Abdfilip was climbing olive trees to sing and play his motets or his arcane, tumultuous tunes that spread all around, from crag to crag, from treetop to treetop. According to others, the old man was looking for mossy holes and for air currents that traveled downward, at times becoming small whirlwinds. They said that, believing that he could not be heard in those caves, he, stretched out on the ground, played to his heart's content, evoking the semblances of Donnanè that he thought were roaming everywhere. They also said that he was trying to capture them and skillfully weave them through the various holes of his instruments. The only thing we managed to establish with certainty was that, in the vanity of the vanities of things, Abdfilip played now one, now the other of the two flageolets he had made for himself, increasing or reducing their vibrations according to the effects he wanted to obtain.

He had one reed that played delicately and as if for fun. Then waves of wafting melodies could be heard at the most unthinkable times, so that it was said that pastures swelled and spikes very slowly formed, while the first butterflies dotted the slopes, and sluggish frost melted in dark caves.

Hearing those stories, Yahin would cover an ear with his hand and retort, "Have you all gone mad? What do we have around us besides boredom and wind, or a few rain showers that April is still bringing us?"

To confirm what he asserted, he would look out from the natural balcony of the Castle as if to capture the slightest noise.

Too many clues, however, supported the story concerning Abdfilip. Once Rowley, returning from his campsite in order to keep in contact with those who had remained, heard musical strains that converged on him from various spots. And, pausing to listen carefully, he thought that invisible beings were playing music in the trunks of the olive trees.

The rumors continued to be confirmed by the different types of sounds, as I have said, that pushed light materials throughout the countryside.

Some said that the other flageolet expressed a language that was less fluent and not as rapid; it was always related to the direction of the sun, the occasional fogs of the Wadi Hamm and the very white rock crystals found along the way.

At such times the flageolet quivered with doleful ebbs and flows, and the resultant collision of atoms provoked sleepiness. A solitary turtledove would happen to pause on a bough and a sparrow hawk on a high bank, and the occasional peasants still living in those areas then felt listless and were attracted by the blooming oak and almond trees. Some of Tirtenio's and Totosimic's men had observed that when one heard the flageolet over great distances, buds did not bloom as usual, but seemed to be animated by another inclination. In the meantime, skylarks rarely took to flight, and suspicious peasants incessantly remained motionless against tree trunks and rough stone walls.

The most reliable account seemed to be that of Ibn-al-Atir, the chicory picker, who traveled far and wide through the territories of Qalat-Minaw. He told us that he had met "Abd," as he called him, in the company of a small dog with white fur on its breast, and that together they had eaten bread and goat's cheese.

Abd had told him that he played day and night, resting for a few minutes in the hollows of tree trunks, and that he did that in order to capture the invisible larvae of dreams and thoughts still springing perpetually from the body of our father, because, being essentially musical principles, they blended particularly well with the sounds of his reeds.

"What are you trying to say?" shouted Yahin, turning to Abn-al-Atir, the chicory picker. "Have you suddenly gone mad?"

But the chicory picker continued speaking impassibly, all the while arranging the greens he had picked into a great number of small bunches.

And he said that Abdfilip chose the most suitable moments of the day for his work, connecting his memories of Donnanè with the reflections coming from herbs and tremulous minerals. That is why he needed two flageolets: one to reproduce the changing emotions of our father (essentially a very mild man), perceiving through vague and airy melodies a mirror of very fresh and serene waters; the other to capture a rugged, almost furious stretch of land, or certain melancholy transits from day to night.

Atman listened to Ibn-al-Atir's account and, strolling, he thought of something else, certainly not enchanted by the voice of the chicory picker, which was somewhat harsh and rough. Uncle Pino, in his disbelief, bit his fingernails, with big Orlando beside him, who delighted in feeling immersed in an ultimate mental conversation with his departed brother.

The chicory picker went on, continually making bunches with the greens. He said that at that point Abdfilip, with his experiments, managed to distinguish the visible attributes of smells and the size of objects, and to feel the incredible appearance with which these things filled the space all around with imperceptible changes in the light. Totosimic cut in, stating that one would not find the origin of things in vegetable gardens, in the landings of rivers and in the thinnest wisps of air but, rather, down below, in the bowels of the earth, in a stratum composed of both iron and nickel splinters.

Ibn-al-Atir continued speaking. He said that everything was possible, now that we had upset the old natural order. His clever arguments were not sufficient to convince us that everything reproduces itself or, turning around and gaining new strength from cause to cause, finds itself to be entirely the same substance.

But when evening fell, many of our men went away, some taking the path of ihc cliff, others the little road overlooking the roofs, all a bit disturbed by the great number of errors that the illusions of sight and heart had made us commit in a short span of time. Some had already learned from Atman that it would be necessary to leave the moon behind, go beyond its nightly orbital path and travel farther into the wheel of the firmament to seek our father-who-was.

But Ibn-al-Atir remained with Mansur and with Lucrezio, who were silently sitting cross-legged in a circle, waiting for Abdfilip's solitary song to rise from the valley and pleasantly shorten the journey of the earth in the heavens.

X

How could earth, water, air and fire still interest us, now that Atman had brought us into the spell of the planetary circles whose movements and dimensions we were forced to study instead of focusing on planes, plants and the limited sublunar world?

We met again on the esplanade of the Castle. There, Atman, strolling with bowed head as usual, explained to us that, according to Albumasar, the leader of the scholars, and to Hubble, Jafar and Eddington, the moon was absolutely of no value to us, nor could it be of any help in our investigations since it was a wall of electromagnetic waves, deep caverns, reddish garnet and, according to some, the sound of a lyre that dulled our senses and would never allow us to distinguish error from truth.

We remained there in silence, some of us dismayed, others pensive and still others ready to intervene.

Pino and Totosimic stood up to defend their views, and Tirtenio got ready to speak to us of the seas as natural shells where everything originates and flourishes. But then Atman said that our conjecturing had not ended nor could it end, because the astronomers were proposing the destruction of the moon—a thing not easily accomplished. Their goal was to obtain a large, inert black hole in the sky, a point, that is, without sense or direction, a night-night-night which we would simply go into with our calculations.

Mansur disagreed with Atman, saying that we would be setting out, from confusion to confusion, on an unknown path of stellar islands and distances that would make the solution to our problem more elusive. As he saw it, our travel amid lunar maps, through angles, ellipses and jagged mountains, had been useless.

The least satisfied was Totosimic, who did not like the abundance of light that reached us from up above because he was thinking of the core of the earth and its abysses. He confused the stars, so to speak, with the lights of the towns that regularly appeared on the northeastern corner of the island, at the foot of Etna and, higher up, on the ridges and cliffs, where they lined up now smaller, now larger, in tremulous blotches. But if one ran his eyes down the slopes of the sky, one immediately encountered those tiny lights that were lost and clustered at the shores of spring torrents and on the arching twigs of broom plants and brambles. But he decided not to insist so as not to discourage Tirtenio and Geber, who were unsure of the goals to be attained, each focusing on different universes, where, according to them, our father's wandering traces could be found in a more concentrated form.

However, Atman cut them short, asserting that the fringes, the rotations and the funereal ballads of the thanatobird had undoubtedly besmirched and disturbed the celestial paths.

Pursuing Eddington's train of thought, it was first necessary to resolve the enigma of the planet Mars, which we saw rising to the west at nightfall and reverberating on the Ionian Sea.

Rowley was happy because, in leaving bulrushes and asphodels, we could lift our eyes amid very distant fireflies and whorls of atoms that made one dizzy from the height and void.

Nergal, Al-Hakim and Lucrezio were distracted by the rumors about Diofar, and they gave little credence to the idea of floating coverings that could have been diverted to Mars by the passage of the extraterrestrial bird, and to that of frost that covered the Martian poles in large white patches.

Everyone looked at the planet from different angles. There were those who saw smoke rising before midnight near the region of Hellas, in the Lake of the Sun, or in the Bay of Alba and in the Fountain of Youth; and everything rotated hour after hour amid strange clouds wandering in red tides.

From our group there arose a great confusion of sighs and words when icecaps and dark intersecting strips of land stood out on Mars. All of that, it goes without saying, appeared in a floating mass of shrubs, animals and crops that, because of our sleepiness, we projected high, up there, in twisted ridges and in eroded plains.

"Oh, how tired I am!" Orlando exclaimed, forced, against his habit, to spend the night out-of-doors to observe the asteroids Pallas, Vesta, Juno and Ceres, which occasionally obscured our view.

The repeated contemplation of such boulders arranged all around Mars, and occupying a stretch which we erroneously estimated to be five or six arms in length, did not displease Rowley and my brother, Salvat.

"When will we finish?" asked Yahin.

Realizing that Atman's intention was to bring us outside our common visible borders, Pino asked,

"What's our destination?"

Each of us had a task: to jot down celestial signs, loops and squiggles, or to spread out maps in order to track down the lost traces. And some, like Lucrezio and Orlando, in an effort to get less tired, looked with a squint at those lights and those whorls in which dust and pebbles were continuously grinding and polishing one another.

In that way, every evening, at nightfall, we explored the latitudes of Jupiter, a slightly golden disk covered with dark bands and gray-blue caps. In it, Nergal, to amuse himself, imagined that there were some embroidered trees; they were divided in as many rows of fronds, which in various positions joined one another, crossed one another and went back to groves of human wood.

Rowley pointed out semiliquid waterfalls and had himself transported there on feluccas, with Mansur at his side, who saw traces of the thanatobird in the lazy, sonorous vessels of the planet.

So, fortunately, we were distracted from the eruptions of that planet and its tyrannical power, which chained us with metals and gases in the circuit of those cold asteroids.

"Patience," said Orlando, wiping his sweat.

With our faces continually turned upward, we passed through infinite degrees, from the heaviness of our body to the lightness of fire, bound now to Venus, now to Mars and Mercury and, farther up, to Jupiter, Saturn and fleeing Pluto. In brief, comforted only by the nocturnal scents that rose up toward us from the valleys of

Qalat-Minaw, we looked out windows wide-open in space, unable to find a solution to our problem.

Pino continued to ask,

"But what's our destination?"

In fact, we had arrived at the limits of the solar system, through many magnitudes of light, exhausted from our sleepless nights, buried and unburied at will by streams of splitting granules and by forges of fine dust.

When dawn arrived on the thresholds of the earth, we stretched out our arms absentmindedly and clumsily, thereby driving away images of dark holes and starry slopes.

We would still have continued traveling in our stellar galleon, with Rowley and Atman at the helm, rushing from center to center toward the unseizable bird, if Diofar's fate, which was very important to us, had not become uncertain, and if Aramea's destiny had not, despite ourselves, aroused a feeling of tenderness in a few informed peasants, in the pikes that swam the torrents and in the listless butterflies.

XI

Nergal had left us to examine the grafted carob with his two assistants. On his return he told us that the recent rains, the winds blowing upstream and the cold still lingering in the nearby woods and meadows had worsened the condition of Diofar, who was now neither tree nor spirit. In no respect was he like what he had been, having been reduced to a gluey form slightly veined by a very thin network of leaves. Unfortunately, since putrefied elements had been deposited on the branches exposed to the humidity of the north, insect larvae found their natural shelter in the carob's wood, and one could see them hatch and grow together with earthworms, termites and misty vapors. It was not a case of unhealthful elements that had precipitated from above or that had been purposely introduced by us, but of red eggs and small worms generated by the season with thousands of antennae and fragile shells. This occurred not only on the chosen tree but in the underbrush of the Wadi Hamm's olive groves, where crickets, locusts and blue wasps were also reproducing.

All this had not helped Diofar, who had developed the wrinkles of bark and of vegetal substances, without the slow renewal of his cells being able to follow the evaporation of the waters and the appearance of lights and shadows all around him. According to Nergal, who spoke while sitting on a linden, if we did not prevent the continual growth of worms with their silken threads that proliferated among the shoots, this condition could not help us in any way.

Nor was it enough to cut the antennae of the crickets being born and the legs of the beetles, or to burn a great number of swallowtail nymphs, and finally to make the graft turn green again with luminous lacquers and drops of quicksilver.

We listened to him in silence, and Rowley smiled with that perpetual pipe in his mouth.

But the plan must have already been prepared with Atman and perhaps with Aunt Agrippa, whom no one ever saw.

Nergal, Drop-of-blood, stated that we should not allow the fragile blooming buds and the small snails encrusted on Diofar to wither, because otherwise, with our errors and illusions, we would risk destroying the missing link between man and the vegetal world. It was foolish to place the so-called maternal instinct before the possible success of our enterprise, which consisted in the search for the flying flame and our father. Even if we were to respect such a sentiment and exalt it with deferential language, we would obtain nothing, since the animal-vegetal shoot was the prisoner of cocoons and seeds, and of the eggs of grasshoppers and scorpions. The blue stains and purple gnarls that covered it hardened that part of the carob and, below the surface, brought it to putrefaction in a swarm of minute animal papillae.

Rowley had grasped his friend's thought and smiled. Uncle Pino ruffled his white hair. Orlando, knitting his thick eyebrows, said,

"What do you want, Nergal?"

Nergal observed that plants produce seeds and fruits, and do not distress themselves like flying and slithering creatures. Instead, they rise very erectly in the sun, fleeing harmful airs and, with invisible motions, avoiding unhealthful sidereal rays.

Losing the consistency of wood, they are reborn as true flowers, and they rise up from the ground with white bordered stems and cones and, outside our narrow confines, with the scattering of sound and light that ineluctably follows the expansion of all bodies and all planets.

Orlando said:

"O Nergal!"

The latter climbed down from the linden. Then, pointing eastward to meadows and forests which had already begun to light up, and turning over some beetles slowly climbing up the stems of camomile plants, he showed us those red insects and their tenuous images reflecting on the stems. He concluded that we would achieve nothing even if we continued for thousands of years to move in a closed circuit of small legs, tiny yellow butterfly wings, truculent faces and men's talons. Mansur sighed,

"From abyss to abyss."

"No," replied Drop-of-blood.

He said that we should save Diofar and not make him go awry in other insignificant lives. We should nourish him with the introduction of soothing sentiments and a new beating heart, which would keep him from being attacked by horrid worms, thereby reintroducing him into the sphere of the aurora borealis and the realm of the planets.

Atman was looking at him from atop a pile of stones.

How else can we save him, continued Nergal, if not by joining him with multiple bonds to the lightness of his mother, Aramea, who, rising up with him in the same environment of leaves and branches, would be giving him a shape?

No one had anything else to say. The conclusion was unexpected.

And Nergal said, "What better shield is there for protecting Diofar and making him live again? What brighter lamp can there be for the night of the transplanted child? What more could she desire, this mother who, out of her mind, ran through towns and valleys followed by ravens that expected her to die imminently, and by goats, hedgehogs, butterflies and gnats that, hearing the beating of her heart, danced slowly around her, all the while protecting themselves in her scanty, trembling shadow?

She was sitting, as I have said, at the foot of a hill, having lost not only her strength but also the softness of her forehead and eyes. Her hands were limp, and she displayed great suffering throughout her body, which toward evening became luminescent with greenish hues in the occiput that flared up when maternal emotions tormented her. Suddenly Emanuele and Muslim, covered with tadpoles and seaweed, and followed rapidly by Ziritia, Mariela and Gheorghy, happened to emerge from the nearby torrent, that is, from the Wadi Hamm, which sprang from that mountainous area with rocky bends and submerged grasses, and spread to the clay stretches and hilly offshoots of the Qamutan plateau.

"Hey you!" they called out.

The woman did not hear them, but as soon as she saw them before her, she smiled, and the children told her that what is heavy on land is light in the waves, where the bark of a cork tree, pikes and air bubbles do not sink to the bottom as happens on land to whatever falls, but rise on paths of water that makes their shapes swell.

"We're speaking to you," said Ziritia.

Aramea smiled again. Muslim, doing a few somersaults, took out of his pockets some butterfly wings, black crab eggs and iris bulbs; Ziritia, blowing on a reed, emitted a sound that made the woman lift her head; and Mariela, using her fingers, wove gold threads and raw silk from silkworms. Gheorghy descended the slope nimbly and, lowering himself into the torrent, swam like a big fish, of course in a deep current. Moving his head, he made his way through the algae and the waves, while Emanuele, who climbed up a holm oak, sang to beguile the turtledoves that approached with merry flight. Aramea felt she was being reborn. With a following of animals and insects clustered at her heels, she lifted her face skyward to catch the long, bright rays of the sun. Then a watchful eagle appeared high in the sky, covering the river with its shadow.

Gheorghy, Mariela and Ziritia plunged into the Wadi Hamm, descending to its deepest spots. Muslim and Emanuele looked at the thousand streaks with which the bird marked the sky above. Seeing the bird hovering above them, they used a willow bow to shoot small arrows which looked like filaments of smoke in that uninhabited region. The arrows soon bent because of their reduced velocity, making them fall downward. The children tried again, employing their strength and shrewdness, and they climbed up an oak tree around which the eagle circled as it continued to maintain itself aloft.

"Hey you!" cried out Gheorghy, poking his head momentarily out of the river. "Have you gone mad? Do you want to be snatched up?"

Ziritia squealed, giving them to understand how imminent the danger was, and despite this, the two children on the tree shot their arrows, which gravity brought down on the stones and dry shoots.

And when the bird, folding its wings, used its weight to descend toward the oak tree, Emanuele and Muslim, saying to the woman "goodbye, goodbye," descended into the torrent and, swimming along the bank and the rough horsetails, disappeared under the water, leaving behind large patches of white foam. The eagle continued to rise for a few seconds, and then, gathering in its feathers, again descended in gray spirals toward Aramea.

"Why don't you return to Qalat-Minaw?" said Al-Hakim, having left the back of his mount. "Everyone is waiting for you."

In those encounters he undermined all the more the body and spirit of the young woman, who lost thickness and shape, having been weakened by the infusions of wine, chopped hemp and black poppy that Al-Hakim administered to her.

"Drink," he said. "It's alkahest."

Not everyone was in agreement over the graft, not so much because of the loss of a life now doomed to perdition but for fear that nature itself could not accept that human-wooden combination which would make us all the more forget the meaning and dimensions of our problem. Therefore, the above-mentioned graft was done without the knowledge of Pino, Mansur, Tirtenio, Totosimic and me.

Aramea was informed of her son's fate by Al-Hakim, and at first did not understand it, reduced as she was to a frail bodily constitution. But waking up suddenly from a deep sleep brought on by herbal teas, she became restless and, hearing the sounds of horns around her, the rustle of palm trees and the running of gazelles, she could only say that her heart was of immense help to her son, and that no one could stop her, not even the imperturbable moon nor the fires that burned every night on the mountains. She wanted to become immortal in the infinite through Diofar, who was waiting for her beyond sunrises and sunsets.

And the young woman ran through the fields, stringing, in her flight, herbs and flowers, clouds and leafy garlands. Meanwhile, from the bottom of the valley, the evening fog arose, scattering in a thousand directions, and a haze strangely appeared that darkened the countryside so that the animals curled up under rocks and amid the wheat earlier than usual.

From the esplanade of the Castle, which already was almost dark, Mansur looked at the chimneys, roofs and windows of the silent town and felt an indescribable turmoil as never before. He said that there could be many generative seeds inside and outside our territories. He remained there motionless, all doubled up.

Aramea, from what we learned, had no rest for several nights. Drenching herself in brine and odors, she called her son until she was overcome with sleep near the carob where Diofar was dying in tiny leaves and black buds. Exhausted, she slept beside him, with a gush of branches and river water at her feet.

I cannot tell you exactly when the transplantation of the woman into the tree occurred, nor did we pay much attention to that, engrossed as we were in our voyage amid the stars and in what the peasants were secretly plotting against us.

The only thing we were told was that everything went well, and this delighted Nergal and his two assistants in that within a short time the carob and Diofar had dampened the scales and the small, moss-encrusted plates, and a regular animal-vegetal development was, therefore, in prospect. Aramea was in a daze and vaguely realized, seized by great happiness, that the moment had come for her to leave a shattered world behind. Nothing of its opaque life interested her anymore since she had lost her knowledge of suffering. She had immediately withdrawn into her sappy existence, being neither woman nor tree but in the process of being transformed in a single circulation with her son.

Nergal informed us that from what had been observed, one could say that it had been a successful operation. There was green flesh and clusters of leaves that would soon overtake the mother-son concrescence with a bunch of red flowers incarnated on the branches in a mixture of pistils and anthers. And at the end of this cycle of leafy development, one would be able to distill the purplish drops of the mother and the white ones of Diofar. But the scent of the flowers of both would be very similar: fragrant hyacinth, scarlet rose and the blossoms of the prickly pear. And the acidulous taste of their most tender vines would attract a great number of birds, so that the carob would have a languorous spring.

An old woman named Cheràstrata, with hair on her breasts, approached us after having returned from hunting for snails and edible mushrooms in the woods. She said that if the event were to be found out, we would attract the wrath of the gods, unless we purified that place, where the soil, the water and the air were infected.

XII

In the infinite deluge of fantasies and afflictions in which the lights of our bewildered minds were being extinguished, it was necessary to find a plan of research that could lead us to the traces of our father and the imaginary bird in the fluxes of stellar protons. But several of our men employed all their knowledge to search elsewhere, as did Tirtenio. The latter denied that the thanatobird had made sidereal rays fall to earth. He had an original idea, namely, that our father's lost semblances lay in the domain of maritime routes and oceanic abysses. Having deliberated privately during some sleepless nights, he left us after a discussion, telling us that he wanted to find primary causes outside the astral circuits. He said he wanted to go with his team through immense seas, discussing the many wonders and telling fantastic stories about the outcome of our adventure.

"I'll return shortly" he said.

So he left us. We followed him from the brow of the crag, while he, turning around, waved a piece of lunar map as if to make fun of us. Then he became smaller and smaller as he proceeded along his way, fading into hazy colors and ever softer sounds.

"So be it!" said his brother Pino. "Do we want to stop on account of this?"

That same evening we resumed our celestial journeys along illuminated roads deformed by the reciprocal magnetic action that, leaving behind the belt of our planets, ineluctably projected us into the magma of the constellation of Hercules.

Then one evening, while we entered the spirals of the Milky Way, we heard a soft whistling coming from the acacias of the ravine.

"Nocturnal birds?" wondered Rowley.

Peering into the dark, we saw, among the trees, some small lights that flitted in and out of the foliage. "What's happening?" Orlando wondered. Since those bouncing trails shifted from the ground to the tops of the eucalyptus trees, Pino cried out, "Is anybody here?" Then we heard some quiet laughter, while those lights flickered all the more, and Muslim, whose voice we recognized, said, "The stars! Don't you see them?"

Pino laughed and so did my brother, Salvat.

In this way the children unwittingly became our friends and refused to leave the esplanade of the Castle so long as we remained there exploring and deciphering the contours of comets and stars.

The spiral of our galaxy twisted around itself several times in a vortex of arms, and it was not a simple or effortless task to cut the fluid materials, cancel others and analyze the strangely designed traces. Atman and Rowley delighted in all of this, at that point no longer distinguishing between night and day, but intercepting dust-bearing currents, varying the altitudes and paths of the stars and introducing in them numbers and formulas in which there could certainly be nothing of our father and our past.

All this made Orlando suffer because, for the most part, he was used to vegetable gardens, pastures and the low, solitary walls of animal pens. Geber, on the contrary, had eyes that sparkled all the more and shone amid those bounding waves. To make the empty stellar abysses less gloomy, Pino, Yahin, Bethsam and I amused ourselves with the children, who, believing they had embarked on a boat (some at the prow, others at the keel), followed us, excited and full of curiosity, in those galactic waters. We were not interested in the motions of rotation, precession and revolution that animated the stars and the white comet tails that suddenly hindered our route, so we let ourselves be transported by the crests of the waves at the keel, which, for the most part, were blue, and we heaved a shower of stones in the granular folds of that matter.

Ziritia said,

"What could be more fun than this?"

Mariela, the timid one, held on to her skirt and could only say, "Oh, oh, how gloomy!" Gheorghy was playing a flageolet and was astonished to hear himself there where the red waters of the worlds lashed against the long coastlines, fretting those universes. The jolliest were Muslim and Emanuele, the former black-haired, the latter blond. Extending their hands, they did not think of mountains and valleys (because one felt less weight up there), but taking chips of porphyry and remnants of deep blue atoms, they dropped them into the void. They laughed, seeing them float on infinite stellar lights, where they circulated and recirculated, turning from left to right, until they went off in different directions amid the vermilion glow of the clouds.

And when we were near the nucleus of the Milky Way, Muslim, seeing that immense flower from the keel of the ship, said that in that swollen node he wanted to play for hours with Ziritia and Gheorghy at his side, who with the sound of the flageolets would beguile that night which the stars tinged in purple.

"Lucky you!" said Pino, with reddened eyes. And he looked at the central egg of the galaxy, a bluish, turbulent mass in which, in his moments of sleep, he saw cirrus clouds floating over the dewy gardens of Sicily.

In the heart of our galaxy, we thought we had found the beginning and the root of our story, which could grow or diminish. We could now stop and, if we so desired, sleep on those seething beds of gases and stars in order to extract vital juices and deductions which would restore to us what remained of our father and the thanatobird.

Yahin and Orlando heaved a great sigh, merrily hopping on the stones of the clearing and looking in the distance at the forests of acacia and olive trees. It was a short-lived joy.

The next day, Atman told us that according to Albumasar, the king of the scholars, only the moon, the stars and the suns derive motion from that center, with an appreciable difference of cosmic solstices and equinoxes which from generation to generation of hadrons and baryons appear in belts of fire.

It was necessary to leave those heavenly bodies to their tides, in whose circles they could expand, and to establish relationships of force which would submerge us, thereby protecting us from the invisible bands of radio waves that rotated as they suddenly fell. The news accentuated our bad mood, tired as we were of contemplating a senseless firmament.

In addition, my sister, Welly, who had come to visit us with her little daughter, Mnemosine, told us that we would be able to find our father's traces not in the realms of fish, animals and terrestrial exhalations but in the life and death vicissitudes of atoms whirling through impenetrable heavenly hollows.

That day, Ibn-al-Atir told us, among other things, that after having traveled through deserts, streams and caves, Yusuf, Aramea's husband, was arriving from the suburban cliffs of Qalat-Minaw with his sonorous cart.

The news spread quickly, and the women went out to their balconies, under vines and scanty orange trees. The older women remained at the windows to look at the eastern flank of the mountain; the old men looked out from the chalky promontories and waved their handkerchiefs; and the children left the lanes in swarms to meet Yusuf, who was struggling along on the curvy mountain road, his cart pulled by a gray horse losing its mane from old age. As was his custom, he was bringing hundreds of strange things from his remote town, and he attracted people's attention because of the plumes he had put on his horse's head, and because of the shining bells. That is why Muslim, Emanuele, Ziritia, Mariela and Gheorghy also left us that morning to head for the clay stretches of the valley.

"Goodbye," Muslim said to us. "Why continue to count the stars? What's the use?"

And fleet-footed Ziritia said,

"Dry yourselves like anchovies under the heavens. Goodbye."

Yusuf's arrival in itself did not interest us, because he could not have easily found out about the transformation that Diofar and Aramea had undergone, but it worried us because of the suspicious peasants, whose bad mood was increasing, and who, with pre-established signals, constantly communicated our movements and decisions to one another. Orlando observed,

"The last thing we needed was this arrival! It complicates every-thing."

Rowley would not hear of this but urged us to plunge again into the tiny particles and the gusts of starry aggregates.

"Do we really want to pay attention to a poor devil?" he grumbled.

That poor devil was making his way up the hill toward Qalat-Minaw, and already many had joined him, greeting him with shouts of "Welcome!" or with reeds that resounded in maddening confusion. He greeted those who met him and, pulling his old horse by the reins, stopped in order to display and give away the knickknacks filling his cart: cuttlebone pendants, red amulets, yellow flageolets, toasted chick-peas and pieces of coral.

"So many things!" exclaimed Mariela.

Yusuf smiled and asked about Aramea—how she was, what she was doing—but nobody knew his wife because she was not from Qalat-Minaw, whereas Yusuf had spent his youth there.

"Who is Aramea?" some woman asked.

And an old man said,

"Are you sure you have a wife with such a name?"

The young man smiled and, running his hand over his black beard and sprinkling small amounts of gold dust on the road, displayed some topaz necklaces and few small amphoras containing vapors of cirrus and rain clouds.

The children marvelled and, asking him for carob seeds, corn, and coconut fibers, secretly got into the cart and opened some of his bottles.

"No, no," said Yusuf to Muslim and Emanuele, who had entered under the canvas top. "This is not the time."

But the deed was done. Out of three amphoras came wisps of clouds and fog which, because of their lightness, rose high in the air and happened to be carried by the breezes of the valley into a small almond grove, edging it with black.

In brief, the entire town had a good time, but nobody could furnish any news about Aramea and Diofar. And the old folk kept asking,

"Are you sure this wife of yours exists?"

Yusuf thought that this was all a joke and waited for our relatives to give him some information about his wife and his son. Meanwhile, in his cart, he arranged large handkerchiefs on strings, and in other places he set out silver spools, green diamonds and shells made of quartz and mother-of-pearl. The women watched him from the lanes. Two magpies sprang from the wheels of the cart to its sides, and the young man, calling them with a whistle, gave them barley and some canary grass seeds.

Going from neighborhood to neighborhood, down streets scarcely practicable because of the mud and dung, he asked about Aramea and his son, but everyone, with voices first clear then tired and weak, told him that they knew nothing. Yusuf grew sad and in the courtyards he collected streams of stellar light to keep merry and to sleep in an aquamarine whiteness on his cart.

Traveling constantly through the same circuit of dead-end streets, potholes and low houses cracked by dampness, he kept asking about his wife until he decided to follow some frightened villager up to the Castle, where, he had been told, they were plotting against the order of the world.

It seems that he spent the entire night looking through the ivy, impressed with our observatory: astrolabes, reddish maps, candles lit in vases, resounding and dazzling radio waves that struck the roofs of the houses down below.

Without being seen, he returned once again to the clearing, where he hid among the dead branches of the plane trees. And hearing that we were traveling in a boat down roads millions of paces long, where, in comparison to the "infinite" number, ten thousand or hundred thousand sandy dunes without a horizon were few or many, he preferred to believe the clever peasants. According to them, we were trying to dislodge and pluck the moon from the sky in order to keep its rays from reaching Diofar and Aramea, they too searching caves and fields for the funereal remains of our father's mind.

Our uncertain travel did not permit us to follow the moods of our fellow townsmen, who could not rejoice or feel assured because of our fallacious proposals.

Ibn-al-Atir, who accepted our provisions and was spending time with us, informed us of the turmoil which had mostly beset the women. After secretly shadowing us during our explorations of the galaxies, Yusuf retraced his steps and, pounding on windows, woke up the shopkeepers, the cart drivers, the cobblers, their women, the young folk, the tailors and the fools, in order to ask them about Aramea and his son, Diofar. But no one was able to tell him anything. Then the townsfolk, losing their tempers because their sleep had been interrupted, got up and went to the rocks and ditches scattered about the town. They went there to appease that man, whose trail could easily be found because of the fog and the smells of sulfur and amber he left behind.

The old men, by then already awake, sat on the balconies, and the more decrepit, in bed to smoke a hookah. And so Qalat-Minaw fumed with tobacco and breaths. The cart drivers prepared their tools, animals and carts in the darkness; the old women lit their ovens with flaming branches beside the young women who were kneading dough; and the barbers, covering their faces with their umbrellas so as not to be recognized, opened their shops and with lights on their doors attracted the night-wandering customers who were following Yusuf.

The noise increased because of the great number of people who, coming from every direction, met as they passed each other, asking about the moon and Aramea, the scholars and our father. Those who were similar banded together, quite soon speaking of streams, seeds, mountains and the colorless night. Rowley looked down at the neighborhoods of clustered houses, on the overpasses and in the tangle of trees, but, despite himself, was unable to follow the divergent paths of the stars nor the solitary fixity of the constellations.

Geber said,

"Something's got to be done! They're plotting against us."

Pino and Orlando wanted to suspend our meetings and continue them with a deeper study of our ideas in another place, such as on secluded mountains. Bethsam was against this idea, and Totosimic proposed an operation in the hollow underground where basaltic rocks and water-bearing strata follow their concentric paths and form a nucleus that cannot be penetrated by light or sound.

In brief, we were unsatisfied, reduced as we were to nibbling at traces of an eternity in flight. Driven back to a state of inertia, we waited impatiently to rid ourselves of all ambiguities.

Uncle Pino grumbled,

"What shall we do? Admit that what the villagers are saying is true?"

One evening, a ring of the waning moon remained, leaving a pale white flux on the lake waters, the few willows of the torrents, the wooded summits and the valleys. We succeeded in obtaining some information about what had happened that evening from Lucrezio, the carpenter. This fellow, when half-drunk, would go from treetop to treetop, even at night, being attracted by the aroma of buds that had recently blossomed and by the very faint chirping of sleeping birds. And from that height he could look out over a great stretch of the surrounding landscape.

"Tomorrow they will head for the mountains of Arcura," he said one morning.

He was smiling and we did not understand whether he too, influenced by Aunt Agrippa, shared in the desire for infinity that the peasants tried to achieve by means of the lunar star that always sets and always reappears in the zodiacal belt of the firmament.

Mansur brought us other news too, because, looking old and being shabbily dressed, he could easily mix in with the crowds that roamed about the countryside during those days.

In brief, we learned that Yusuf, bewitched by the idea of finding Aramea in some lunar fold where he imagined her exhausted because of the red deserts she had crossed and, wanting to collect the small heart of his son in the seaweed that reflected the very distant sign of Scorpio, dragged along almost all the inhabitants of the sparsely populated Qalat-Minaw.

"Patience!" said my brother, Salvat. "It's our fault. We should have worked in a grotto, unseen by anyone."

And Rowley, lighting his pipe, said,

"It'll pass."

However, the peasants, the old women, the children and some goats and stray dogs headed for Arcura and the hill of Carratabbía, whose rocks stood out toward the northeast within a sparse vegetation where, in addition to wormwood, which easily breaks up into corymbs, the very strong scent of rue prevailed.

There were probably many of them, perhaps two or three thousand, because that evening by chance, during a moment of rest, we heard an unusual murmur coming from along the lands of Nunziata and rising up to the Castle.

According to Lucrezio, the crowd walked in two files, women and men, and Yusuf preceded them with the boy, Emanuele.

"Tonight we'll take the moon," said Yusuf; and the people followed him down many paths and along the uneven and bumpy turf.

He had told everyone (after having interpreted certain conjectures we had expressed) that we intended soon to uproot the satellite from the sky.

It was not easy to climb up toward Carratabbìa because of the rocky terrain and because the path was covered with capers and myrtles which the older folk grabbed onto in order to climb with less effort.

They circled the mountain from the left, the youngest, followed by the goats, scrambling up the above-mentioned paths.

At this point Lucrezio told us that they all went toward the summit, that is, onto the ridge, through scrub, wild olive trees and very ancient tombs hewn out of the rock. Mansur, with summary gestures, gave us to understand that only Yusuf and Emanuele had gone onto the crag of the mountain.

He had noticed this from the sudden silence and the dark clusters of men and peasant women that covered the slopes of the hill. The old folk said in a whisper,

"Silence!"

Yusuf was carrying a golden plate which was neither large nor small. After having passed it from one hand to the other, he gave it to the boy before arriving at the rocky clearing of Carratabbía, from which one could see a panorama of the nearby lands. According to Yusuf, at that moment one could observe or divine what was essential in all things as long as we fled the anger and perverse thoughts of Atman, Albumasar, Zephir, Salvat, Eddington, Jafar, Rowley, Totosimic, Geber, Orlando and my sister, Welly. He spoke of the principles of moss, sapphire and civet, and of the natural scents that would grow stronger as the waning moon approached the rim of the mountains; especially rue, which sprouted in fissures distinguishable in the dark.

Mansur said that Yusuf was an impostor because he used arcane tricks to deceive and win over the peasant crowds. But according to Lucrezio, Yusuf, not having found Aramea and Diofar, wanted our satellite to perish because of its very advanced age and because a great number of atoms in the form of light beams had abandoned its surface and its mountains.

It was a cool evening, owing in part to the frost forming in the granaries of the valley and in the nearby hills, and so the people covered themselves with shawls or took shelter in the canebrake located near a large grotto.

"Oh, come now," someone said. "When are you going to start?"

But we could not start until that waning crescent moon arose, its thin horns, vaguely surrounded by a purplish white veil, embroidering the tops of the mulberry bushes, the very few cypresses and the shining rocks.

From then on we received very little news because Yusuf and the boy were seen only once up there, and Emanuele stood there with a plate stretched forth toward the horizon, trying to capture and multiply what came unaltered from the sickle of the satellite. The peasants whispered,

"Will they manage to catch it and save it?"

They waited until late that night when even some goats happened to arrive in Carratabbìa and, desiring sleep, had curled up with their heads pressed against their hairy sides. (Some said they had been purposely driven toward Nunziata to provide warm milk in case of a prolonged wait.)

In the countryside the shadows faded quickly, and nothing hindered them because the visible stars, which looked like a continuous bustle of corpuscles in the air, were very distant. Then Yusuf spoke for the last time from the deserted hill. He stated he would save the moon so that it would add vigor and growth to the spikes, the invisible seeds and the various flowers that subtly perfumed the voluble night; and also so that it would navigate on the sea waves and on the bushes tied and made into bundles; and especially in Qamut, where the shadow of earth, water, very thin air and fire, in their oscillating movement, penetrated the nature of things that come into existence and perish.

Lucrezio and Mansur, however, gave contradictory reports concerning what I have related above.

It was thought that what remained of the moon at daybreak occupied continuously less space, while on the head of the boy there was a scattering of faint lunar reflections, and down below, the people in the canebrakes and in the clearing in front of the grotto looked up.

Many of them were tired because they had spent the night out in the open.

From the ridge of the mountain, where heavy dew was collecting, and where they huddled together to protect themselves from the cold, they listened to Yusuf.

It was impossible to make out what he was saying while he stretched his arms along the lunar arc. Therefore, I will relate the testimony of Ibn-al-Atir, the chicory picker, who had sharp ears, being used to distinguishing even the slightest rustling sound that herbs make underground when they are growing.

It seems that Yusuf also spoke of shadows, and then of roaming twisted corpuscles, interspersing senseless sentences, or so they appeared because the summit of Carratabbìa was in the distance. And he spoke about Tenom, Musach, Motagren, of Domeis, Sgum and about himself, Yusuf, *ut ire invisibiliter possit.*

Lucrezio added that he went on speaking for a long time, perhaps to dazzle the peasant masses, and that he mentioned Succentai, Plinthia, *noctium phantasmata*, and then *phantasmata, phantasmata*.

Several people, at that point, saw him grow taller. The air took on the hues of a great variety of colors, and the moon was truly a tiny speck down there, a single horn of white stone that was slowly pouring into the golden plate, which was shinier than ever, when it became entangled in vines and the scales of branches.

Certainly, from that moment on we learned no more, because everyone in town, late that day, had his own version of the facts. And we heard a great many contradictory opinions. Pino shouted,

"What sort of nonsense is this? Let's get back to our work."

I will only say that some fanatics spoke of asps and basilisks upon which they had walked right after the moon was captured, and others said that this star had been wrenched from the sky by Yusuf and had been set up in some den, fixed and bound to the elytra and the mouth of Aramea (whom no one ever saw again, if not in dreams), and twined around the woman's wrists in a natural way.

For Mansur, that was possible, considering the transmutations we ourselves managed to achieve; and, with gloomy faces, we circled around him, with Rowley, who told him to leave us forever and not to burden us any longer with nonsense, because we did not need odes and chimeras, babel and antibabel, but a rational approach that reduced the hostility of nature to phenomena, graphs and predictable laws.

I should also mention that as soon as the peasants who were scattered about the countryside received the news from Qalat- Minaw, they grew more suspicious, fearing our threats and a flood of calamities.

Informed by Cheràstrata, they learned something of the fate of Aramea and her son, without knowing for certain whether the two had been changed into fragrant wood or encapsulated in the wandering moon and locked up by Yusuf with it in a cave where elecampane grew and an immaterial fire was generated. Others, instead, did not express their opinions, but as they crossed rocky ar-

eas and courses of water, they collected reeds and marsh sedges, and after having climbed up to the high crags, they exposed them to the blue residues of the lost moon.

Still others, finally, chose to find the scales of the moon, and they followed the scents that Yusuf left in his trail as he busily analyzed the saltiness and weight of the winds to find his bride and his son. As we shall see, he learned something about those two from Muslim.

XIII

Nergal would inform us daily about the graft. He would tell us what color it was turning, describing the great variety of black and green that made it stand out under the high nocturnal lights. He also described the hybrid cells within the carob that quickly produced flowers and fruits with ambiguous appearances.

And he invited us to go down to see and celebrate the novel beauty of the graft and the trilobed leaves that covered it, since it was easy to make the duplicated parts, whose appearance could fool the most expert eye, look healthy for about ten seconds.

"Forget the heavens!" he had one of his two assistants say to us. "And come and see the delicate vegetal heads!"

So we went, even if we felt a bit troubled because of the many things that hourly were happening around us. Atman said that the bird's flight zone could best be calculated if we carefully considered what came between that perspective and the transplanted individuals.

We went down in small groups. I was with Salvat and Rowley. The path was dry because the winds in those April days had arrived from south of the valley with low, gentle gusts that skimmed the tops of the oak trees and the chalky terraces of the valley.

"Oh, finally!" said Bethsam, with his rifle slung across his back.

He picked some succulent almonds.

"Eat!" he cried out.

Nergal had locked many birds in a cage to delight us with their singing that, spreading from gorge to gorge and through the subterranean waters, could again be heard on the crests and in the meadows of the lowlands.

"Welcome!" he shouted when he saw us.

Totosimic said to me, "Do you think other misfortunes await us because I'm still with you?"

One could not easily spot the grafted part of the carob because of certain soft protuberances that were even gluey in some spots. Moreover, besides perceiving arboreal incrustations on the mother's and son's limbs, one could see that their eyes had lost their sweetness. One also noticed that the eyes formed long translucent elements which called out to one another with repressed flickers immediately reintegrated in the great mixture of vegetal principles.

"See?" Nergal said. "One can't even make out the junction where the grafting was done."

On those branches, the bark was smoother, not rough, and it was suspended amid the dense growth of the carob.

Nergal, seeing us somewhat perplexed, insisted that Aramea and Diofar had attained a state of rest. He said that they were no longer subject to the laws of free-falling weights but to a spatial orientation that, freeing them from crystalline granite and damp earth, brought them upward in bizarre coils of leaves where nothing clashes frenetically but everything becomes airy and white. Nor were those two beings afflicted with sensations, except for those coming from the whirlwinds, the singing of birds (we had just heard) and the atoms of fog that quickly and easily dissipated.

Small reeds, horsetails and a few meadow saffrons with yellow stigmas had sprouted around the carob from violet-colored mounds.

To relieve us from the confused emotions to which we had fallen prey, Nergal had a table prepared with some boards over the torrent, so that we could simultaneously enjoy the bank, the current and the beautiful day.

"Come now!" he said. "What are we waiting for? Let's eat and then drink a toast! The pine, oak and larch trees, the seedbeds of the insects and the blade-like beams piercing the river tell us to do so! Come!"

Uncle Pino, with his expertise, killed a young goat and, after having punched holes in it with a knife, filled the meat with sharp cheese, pepper, rosemary, potatoes and Vittoria wine.

Mansur had followed us reluctantly and did not speak.

The fire was kindled with juniper and oak fronds. The meat was cooked on a large grate, the smoke slowly spiraling over the gorges of the valley, and when there was a breeze, to the tops of the olive trees. The bread brought by Ibn-al-Atir, who did not fail to attend the banquet, was fresh; it was arranged along the length of the table.

"This is what we should look for." said Yahin. "Let's leave the insects, the clouds and the stars be!"

Rowley, Nergal, Atman, Orlando and Al-Hakim were happy and, between one course and another, proceeded to reexamine the process already described. What is more, they spoke of the modalities of the soul and whether it changes or disintegrates over time. They also spoke of the one and the multiple, wondering whether light shines from us or rather in us.

Since the thighs of young goats are much tougher than those of calves, Lucrezio took the leanest part, cut it into thin slices and dipped it in kidney fat, a few herbs, honeyed wine and some salt, offering it all to us, his table companions. There were also beccaficos killed by Bethsam, pieces of pig's liver, bone marrow and capon breasts.

Every now and then boiling water was poured into the rolling torrent, which was becoming flecked with patches of quivering foam.

Nergal spoke to us of the change that resides in things, and according to him, it was now necessary that we make plans for future animal-vegetal grafts to be made on tree after tree, thereby eliminating the distress and fear that arise in people from their thoughts.

The sun was pleasant and directly overhead. Some swallows were flying around Qalat-Minaw.

Meanwhile, having finished his portions, Lucrezio prepared some strawberries picked in the underbrush and fresh broad beans fried slowly with egg yolks. We drank some almond milk.

Nergal, perhaps stimulated by the wine, was constantly talking. He spoke of a hill in Qamut and of the plains above it where allegedly only men-trees thrived. They were indeed strange, but a perfect example of a new disposition of nature. According to him, we could erect bridges of similar trees in the gray valleys, in the remote frontiers of our land and along the banks of our rivers.

Then he smiled. Atman squinted to see him better. The water of the Wadi Hamm was passing limpidly under our table.

"Understand?" continued Drop-of-blood. "A vegetal-animal world, soft branches that dusk darkens into human inflorescences."

Mansur was following the gestures of the biologist, who had stopped eating in order to mark huge circles and straight lines in every direction as if he was trying to render into vegetal arabesques even the backgrounds of the hilly landscape marvelously rounded by the blossoming mountain plants. The meal lasted a long time. The clear day, still young, gave us joy. Lucrezio, taking advantage of Nergal's moments of silence, told us that there existed a town in which with eight ounces of sugar, some bitter orange rinds, nutmeg, grapes, cloves and pomegranate seeds, and what is more, all that mixed with ground cinnamon, tangerines and some more sugar, one could, with a proper fire and by whipping and stirring, make a pastry such as no human mouth could ever have tasted.

We sat on the grass and on the boulders of the nearby grotto in order to nap a bit at the sound of the Wadi Hamm.

Mansur and Al-Hakim were walking around the carob, which was generally motionless, except for its vermicular movements, that were not always perceptible. Then Atman advised protecting the tree, insulating it from sudden contacts with the surrounding world and from eventual incursions from the unknown.

That is why it was decided to transport ivy from the nearby hills and to wrap it several times around the tree so that its vital part would not suffer any damage, and also to prevent the human component from overwhelming the arboreal one and once again becoming moving limbs and forms in the maze of the carob's sun-seeking fronds.

For this, Nergal proposed planting some peyotl around the tree, a cactus plant not easily found in our parts. It would curb Aramea's and Diofar's excessive growth, leaving them in a state of sleepiness.

"Agreed," said Atman.

None of us opposed the plan since what had happened was irreversible. Moreover, having been distracted by some unexpected incidents, we were little interested, at this point, in the lifeless appearance of the mother and her son. We felt conspiracies and snares forming in our own squads and among our relatives.

As usual, we left one phlegmatic and one melancholic, sheltered in a large stone tower, to serve as watchmen. The former, Ibn-al-Atir, had a thorough knowledge of the area and the nightly migrations of the peasants. During the day, he, dressed in black, watched the tree, its mutations and its wretched development in life. The latter, Kid, one of the melancholics, dressed in red in order to capture the light of feeble stars and to stand out better down there, was supposed to observe the vegetal particles scattering in the air, the roots growing very slowly in the nearby bend in the river and, finally, any possible deterioration of the grafted elements.

We returned to our cosmos, not all of us convinced, with Toto-simic, who, without any apparent reason, appeared somber and began to entertain gloomy thoughts. Atman this time wanted to determine the laws of the original astral numbers and the multitude of galactic years in which, under the action of attracting seas, worlds expand in an interlacement of magnetic effects.

But in the countryside, the peasants were keeping vigil, secretly meeting, and they were already plotting against us, being shrewder than the inhabitants of Qalat-Minaw.

Among other things, what was being communicated to us regarding Aramea and the tree was not always reliable and sure.

Ibn-al-Atir, for example, spoke to us of the fine growth of the peyotl, which was already sending forth its first lilac-colored blossoms eastward and its light brown ones northward. Moreover, he said that mother and son had been grafted well, and had apparently achieved an equilibrium between kinetic forces and molecular inclination. Unfortunately, there appeared large protuberances that interminably repeated the former condition, which had not been completely absorbed in the arboreal structure.

"Well!" exclaimed Yahin, hearing this news.

And Orlando:

"We're spinning our wheels!"

Ibn-al-Atir, an expert in herbs, informed us that Diofar was veg-etatively doing better, perhaps because of the proximity of his mother's heart, which one could vaguely hear beating. It was not like a true heartbeat, since such an occurrence was improbable, but like sudden expansions of the branch immediately absorbed in the wrinkled development of the racemes.

All that would have made us happy because, among other things, we would soon have been able to determine what effect the thana-tobird had on the stars and the air. But the other watchman, Kid, informed us of other aspects of the Aramea-carob being, which was developing and progressing in roads without an exit. The melan-cholic was speaking to us in a soft voice as if he feared he would ruin the incorruptible evening of the Wadi Hamm. He told us that the peyotl, growing in clumps and with small shoots that attacked the tree on all sides, developed a luminescence that sometimes emitted frigid waves and, at other times, faint heat waves. All of the above could easily be seen right after dusk.

"What stories is he going around telling?" joined in Uncl Pino.

Kid defended his thesis, for, in his words, one had only to put a mirror in front of the carob at the above-mentioned times to see green flashes that were instantaneously sent back to the center of the tree.

At other times one saw swift luminous streaks, brusque move-ments of the grafted branches that, with the necessary slowness, headed for the fresh water of the torrent.

In the morning Ibn-al-Atir told us that his companion was not entirely sane, since it did not take much to understand how the tiny lights dancing within the carob were caused by the flight of fireflies that appeared when the stars rose in the heavens. Because of the increased humidity, these flies came from the gorges and the stonecrop proliferating in the woods of the mountains.

All one needed, in fact, was to shift oneself slightly southward (walking cautiously, naturally) or northward, to discover a different perspective, so that dense swarms of fireflies would undergo a strong deviation. And if one shifted southward, they appeared to form other deep-blue islands.

The melancholic did not agree, and he communicated that to us when the chicory picker slept stretched out on a sack, feeling more at ease on the sloping bank of the river.

Looking at the stars, and not at the carob, which had another disposition, said Kid, one could see those brief lights appearing and disappearing from opposite locations, it being a case of changes in the visual angle. Furthermore, very late at night, he heard some sounds that continually followed the same bewitching course.

Nergal wanted to investigate the phenomenon, so for several days he returned to the valley to examine whatever he might happen to see.

After completing his careful inspection, he said that one thing for certain was the fact that Aramea had lost her former nature, having passed into a hybrid state of opposing aggregates.

Yahin interrupted him, observing that we had brought chaos to Qalat-Minaw, and nothing else.

"Quiet!" my brother, Salvat, said to him.

For Nergal, the human-vegetal mixture was still sentient. Having escaped certain natural limits, and enclosed in a small network of sap, arboreal structures and woody shells, it had reversed the vague direction of its characteristics—the direction it still possessed. And who knows how much the peyotl's humors that the soil underground absorbed voraciously further represented such a contact with what was real? In all this there were traces of a forgotten memory that the slightest thing could disturb and that the cactus flowers tormented, because everything coming from the exterior remained dark and indivisible.

In fact, the phosphorescent eyes of an owl, or a small dying star, were enough to make one hear at night, when one rested one's ear on the trunk of the carob, vibrations, now joyful now tender, which gradually assaulted the tree from its roots to its crown; and then, the small branches would bend flexibly at the passage of vibratory vortices, which made the tree appear immersed in thousands of sonorous sistrums.

It was not likewise regarding the noises made by chirping magpies in the bushes, by swarms of gnats, or by frogs in love.

Nergal was not expressing an empty opinion. If we closely examined the tree when it was struck by a wave of vibrations, we would see an extremely faint swarming of colors originating from the human nodes and the hermaphroditic flowers. In short, an inversion of visual and auditory effects was taking place.

This is why the tree was tinged with colors, which were sometimes rapid and spinning, and sometimes impalpable and very minute. For Nergal everything depended on a hidden sensitive faculty and confused feelings, largely extinguished, of love, hatred, fear and kindness which the luminous currents of the sky, earth, and moon arouse in us. Therefore, both Kid as well as Ibn-al-Atir were right, because each of them looked at the human-vegetal nodes in a particular way and at different moments of the day.

For example, because the season was changing, dawn was striking the carob at a tangent, first on its crown and gradually on its soft grafted branches that resounded slightly with an ephemeral rustling.

Fortunately, Nergal concluded, as we sat around listening to him in silence, the Aramea-Diofar substance had escaped the realm of thought, and nothing afflicted it, neither the present nor the future nor its gloomy regression to the past, being mother and son immured in billions of vegetal cells.

Al-Hakim smiled, saying that Aunt Agrippa was correct in stating that everything changes and that nothing has a center. Pino had stood up and, strolling along the esplanade of the Castle, looked at us and then at the surrounding valleys as he repeated,

"I'm beginning not to understand anything about anything!"

To better protect the carob, we decided to pack around it some red tufts, cocoons of butterflies and other insects, an arm of the torrent (diverted to the rear), papyruses, and bird nests full of eggs, so that from a distance it would all look like a hotchpotch of herbs, beetles and flowers.

XIV

Unfortunately, the story of the Wadi Hamm's carob spread quickly. Moreover, the ivy, the tangle of grasses, the bundles of canes and the brocade cloths spread out at night were not enough to shield it from the eyes of the few frightened wayfarers who secretly passed by, or from the vagabond peasants who came from the torrents and chalky lands of Oltretrezzito, poking their faces out from behind the rocks with improvised excuses to see the tree's colors and hear its sounds.

Learning of this, Orlando said that we had to drive the peasants out of those parts, even when they casually passed by on their donkeys or stretched out on the scarp, pretending to enjoy the woods scintillating under the sun. In Salvat's opinion, we needed to do this quickly in order to avoid delaying the attainment of the goal of our explorations in spring watersheds and in the immutable void of stellar spheres.

We would have resumed our ballets amid the white worlds of endless galaxies if sporadic but insistent news about branches, treetops, half-trees and entire almond trees cut down without plausible reason had not reached us.

At first, we paid little attention to this, since we were distracted by the jumble of our astral computations, but when the deed was repeated again and again, and increasingly so from day to day, we sent some of our men around led by Ibn-al-Atir, who had stopped guarding the carob.

Nor could it have been a case of simple pruning, given the ceaseless migration of the peasants, and the season, which was scarcely suitable for that. Indeed, spring was at its apex, turning the stones green over a distance of many kilometers and making the boundary walls of the countryside flower.

"Come now, pay no attention to these things," said Rowley, fascinated by the streaking comets and the heavenly fires.

Uncle Pino added,

"One should burn the peasants alive. They're always coming up with something or other."

It was Cheràstrata who made us understand what was happening. The old woman, walking with a lazy gait and avoiding prickly thistles, came from the Washhouse to meet us.

"Hey you," she said when she saw us, "would you like to buy some peppery mushrooms? They're small and fragrant, and were picked a short time ago in the lowlands."

She showed us a basket chock-full of mushrooms with gray stems.

"Where are you coming from?" Orlando asked her.

"From far away."

"Explain yourself."

"From the valley of the Wadi Hamm, where trees no longer rustle merrily."

"What do you mean?" asked Pino.

The old woman put the basket down at our feet. And she said, more with gestures than with words, that the suffering of a tree is not a common thing, nor is it something predestined. Rather, it is the result of a bitter desire to make repugnant what once blossomed with beautiful efflorescences.

The old woman went away. Uncle Pino wanted to question her further and held a willow branch high in the air in an effort to catch up with her.

Going from one strange thing to another, we learned that same day, from the news gathered by Ibn-al-Atir himself, that the peasants were purposely destroying the trees to prevent us from afflicting them with monstrous vegetal-animal appearances.

"I suspected that would happen," Yahin cut in. "And I too am at fault. I've lost my good sense."

At first, it was only on cliffs and in secluded places that olives, pomegranates, holm oaks and other trees growing there were cut down with clever excuses and with calculated indifference; then, simultaneously, in several other places as if to remedy their excessive growth. We knew that the peasants customarily pruned the trees according to the trend of the year. From what the local inhabitants of the place had told us during our moments of rest, the past winter had been dry, with southern winds that portended a rainy spring and an enormous regrowth of buds. That is why we had not paid any attention to the situation. What made it more serious was not so much the felling of an olive tree, or whatever tree it was, but the systematic destruction, in the span of a few days, of hawthorn, medlar, pear, almond and beech trees, even when they were exposed to the west; that is, when they were sheltered from the winds that blow rather violently from the east during those months.

"What are we to do?" asked Orlando, losing his usual patience. "Shall we see destroyed what for years has been cultivated in our territory?"

But it was the carob that Nergal feared would be destroyed. If it had depended on him, he would have protected it with a hundred horses and five thousand foot soldiers equipped with halberds tipped with lanterns.

We were forced to follow the unfolding of the events occurring in the countryside—not an easy task, since we were used to the cadenzas of young extragalactic stars and whatever was flickering on the edges of the nebulae.

At dawn, cold winds blew, if only briefly. It was as if we had gone back in the season. And the sun did not light up our sites before having risen high in the sky. From there, it dissipated the mist and the heavy dew, and many solar elements were thus leaving us and our town, while, down below, torbid, dark vapors were preparing the rebirth of all things. The destruction continued throughout the day. The waters of the torrents were no longer clear because of the leaves and arboreal scales that made them turbid, and also because of the prevalence of fogs that, mixing in with the torrents, blurred their limpidity.

Later we managed to learn from Ibn-al-Atir and Lucrezio that the peasants did not always uproot the trees; instead, they often dug ditches around them, which they made so deep as to allow maple, oak, or olive trees to sink into the ground.

"A clever idea," commented Yahin.

For the most part, they would cover a tree with earth in such a way that its crown appeared on the ground and expanded sideways as if growing directly from the surface. In so doing they thought they might save the olive tree, and other trees, for better times. Or they made some opposing holes from a very low level (from an embankment below, for example), and from there they gave the branches a proper direction, having calculated, in their own way, which wind was harmful and which was healthful. In so doing they also balanced the cold spots with the hot ones. Furthermore, even the short rivulets brought by the season were directed toward the buried tuft, the emerging fronds or the sulfur grass and the first poppies, so that all the waters exposed to the east would be channeled toward the almond, fig and holm oak trees. These waters were fresh, sweet-smelling and uncloudy given the fact that as soon as the sun arose, it could shine in their midst.

"Marvelous! Marvelous!" exclaimed Yahin, visibly satisfied.

Ibn-al-Atir, bringing us such news, added that in being protected like that, the trees maintained their flowers and branches in excellent condition because they were not exposed to the cold winds that blow between the point where the sun sets and that where it rises. And these trees could easily be protected from the hot winds that travel from east to west in continuous currents.

Many peasants hid to avert possible illnesses and the unhealthful conditions that, according to them, brought death and incredible confusion to the flourishing valley of the Wadi Hamm because of the carob, or the disgusting *zaqqum*, as they called it. They chose rocky places where, by digging continuously, they made springs gush forth to quench their thirst. These were limpid and freshwater springs in which the changes of the day dissolved or brought up from down below very minute traces of sulfur, calcium and magnesium, as well as imperceptible particles of iron, silver and gold.

The movement of the peasants was greater than what we had imagined, because they migrated from area to area at the most unthinkable times, exchanging their concerns and plans. From the bottom of ravished hollows, they went up to the summits, and there they looked down to see if others were following them. Forming black assemblages along paths stained with sulfur, they cut down trees and the sprouting bushes of small oaks. Finally, they went from the abandoned houses to the grottos which abound in Qamut. They slept there, only to leave those half-buried hiding places at dawn, or the airy shelters of pine trees left intact atop the hills.

I believe they found it difficult to procure food for themselves, and since they walked at night, they could not with sure hand kill rabbits and foxes on the bare rocks shrouded in darkness. Communications with Qalat-Minaw were sporadic, and in town, furthermore, many did not know of Aramea's fate nor had they ever seen her. The few who knew of it did not think that a body should be mortified in a carob and that objects near it should be thinned out and dispersed.

However, the more fortunate peasants ground some grain, kneaded the dough and cooked it in improvised ovens to make buns.

The majority of them, according to Ibn-al-Atir's and Lucrezio's same account, mixed what was left of the corn, broods of birds and unripe fruit, to make soft loaves of bread, in turn mixing weak foods with strong ones. They excluded the very bitter from the bitter, the very sweet from the sweet and the very sour from the sour. And they exchanged their provisions in meadows and marshes, or they met to discuss and to fell trees, especially at dawn when dew fell and the western winds, still somewhat cold, blew. Those who were more isolated caught butterflies in flight, adding them to the crowns of almond and beech trees, to stray chilled grasshoppers and to honeyed mushes, and they kneaded them with spring water in order not to suffer hunger.

One night we saw fires on the heights of Qamut and, beyond them, in the interior of Inchiodato. Since similar spectacles were increasingly repeated on rocky terraces and in ravines and gorges, with plumes of smoke that rose up against the light amid the olive trees, we realized we had to do something.

The peasants' goal was clear: to get continually closer in order to destroy Aramea and the carob.

Bethsam and Orlando wanted to send some hunters around with shotguns to fire a continuous volley of shots so as to frighten the peasants and make them retreat beyond our territories, through ruinous slopes, mud and low riverbeds. Actually, Nergal wanted to dislodge the men from their holes, peppering their legs with shot, if necessary, in order to drive them into the belt of the coastal plains.

The opinion that prevailed was that of Ibn-al-Atir, who was very clever because of the many, many years he had spent among the peasants and the herbs, willows and mushroom fields of Qalat-Minaw. He left with Bethsam, Lucrezio and a fellow from Totosimic's group, promising us that if we left him well-stocked with bread, olives and cheese, he would free us from the danger posed by the runaway peasants. His plan was very simple, even if it engaged the men for some days in the hunt for eagle, screech, barn and horned owls to be found within high schists, in tangles of nests and even on very tall plane and cypress trees, where those feathered creatures hid.

Bethsam easily found holes and hollows where he caught those birds by their claws. And together with his companions, he quickly hung them, bound with string or wire, to the trunks of trees along the Wadi Hamm's watershed.

"What are they trying to do?" asked Rowley, absorbed in counting stars, which he accomplished by piling up gravel, leaves and scraps of paper.

"Don't you know that at night the peasants, and more so the women peasants, mistake noises for the transmigration of restless, condemned souls?" answered Pino.

The peasants, hearing in the valley a swell of very sad songs that broadened the dimensions of the night, progressively reduced their sorties, leaving the wooded bands and advancing through inaccessible cavities in the rocks immersed in a fixed silence.

Orlando said to us,

"You'll see, they'll resume their raids."

However, both when the air was calm and when there were occasional rains, one heard eagle, screech and horned owls in the darkness.

"Oh!" exclaimed Yahin. "They're weeping guitars and mandolins."

The nocturnal hullabaloo lasted for several days given the strong constitutions of those birds, which endured both cold and hunger. Nevertheless, some trees were still felled in certain gorges and in the mountainous belts. The past and present felling of trees determined sooner than foreseen the flight of fledglings which, in that month of April, were born in thousands of nests on branches, barks, red bilberry bushes and in unused rock quarries.

We had not thought of such an occurrence. It did not displease us, because it could amuse us. Yahin was happy. Orlando's fat cheeks turned red from joy.

It was necessary, furthermore, to keep in mind that the species of creatures being born were quite numerous, since the abandoned countryside of Sicily was able to incubate and give birth to silkworms, millipedes, centipedes, snails, mosquitos, flies and to swallowtails and other butterflies.

All those creatures came and went, tracing brilliant flight patterns as they changed shape and direction. And thronging, dispersing and coming together again, they stole the splendor from the lands, or vaguely overshadowed them with tireless wings.

"Hey, why don't we go in the middle of the meadows?" said Geber, whose frequent bad moods were diminishing. "Who better than us down there?"

The most interesting flights were those of the birds, which sometimes left the fields of broad beans and the few plots of curly chickpeas. Siskins, sparrows and goldfinches flew right down to us, landing indifferently in our presence to find rootlets and lichens among the ruins of the Castle, or to pursue swarms of gnats. Bethsam was enraptured and, pointing to some birds arising from the sunny slopes and the streams we spotted in the distance, told us that they built their nests with mosses, hair, straw and feathers, and on pine, plum, apple and carob trees. He also spoke to us of their sharp eyes, with which they perceived the texture of leaves, pecking at the sweetest of them, or the gushing of a spring from ferns, or insects sleeping in the hollow spaces of sepals and petals, and finally the passing of breezes through Qalat-Minaw's few laurel trees.

In short, these were peaceful days, during which we contemplated nothing more than that resurgent nature. So we found ourselves leaving one another and, with the excuse of wishing to meditate on being and nonbeing, we fell asleep, resting against the trunks of trees or seated amid the dense foliage of their branches.

XV

Having left Mt. Carratabbìa about dawn, Yusuf, followed by the children, went down the opposite slope. And while they all wandered aimlessly through the countryside, he learned from Muslim that the men had seen an unknown woman, whom they had then left near Trezzito.

After asking many questions, Yusuf understood that it was Aramea. He had further evidence from Ziritia when she spoke of a black-haired woman whose ankles were adorned with wind-flowers and yellow seeds. And so, Muslim, Emanuele, Mariela, Ziritia and Gheorghy followed the young man who said that he had removed the moon from the sky forever, overturning it and converting it into extremely fine splinters that could reappear only on weeds, ears of corn and solitary trees, provided that Diofar and Aramea had chosen to recreate them. Mariela laughed and Ziritia asked,

"Will you do the same with the stars?"

But Yusuf, following his train of thought, asked the children to show him the place where they had last seen the woman sitting by a brook.

They cut through the lands of Nunziata on their way back and, going from hill to hill, they arrived at Trezzito, where oak and beech trees were densely massed together. To inform the solitary peasants of their passage, they carved the outline of a heart and that of an infant on the trunks of holm oaks, on the most glittering rocks and on the shoulder bones of goats that had died during their wanderings. And that was not all, because Muslim, leaping from one fork of a tree to another, took wrens, snails and grasshoppers, and, using pine needles, engraved five symmetrical signs and ten eyes on them, which in essence represented the five of them who were pursuing changing terrestrial fantasms. Then Yusuf asked,

"Do you think our journey will be very long?"

We learned for certain from Al-Hakim (who like the rest of us was interested in diverting Yusuf's anxiety toward a false appearance of love) that the youth, not suspecting that the course of the Wadi Hamm was the route taken by Aramea, often avoided it, especially where black boulders made it murky.

Driven to some extent by his temperament, and to some extent by his excitement over the children, he not only inscribed what we mentioned above but, depending on how the day went, revealed the most important events in a few transcribed monosyllables. So one could read on a palm root, "*the hour strikes ceaselessly;*" or, "*water rings in the fissures and calls you;*" or, "*clouds of dust penetrate the soul;*" and furthermore, "*Aramea, mother of the dense swarming stars;*" and in times of discomfort, "*I spent the night atop a lofty observatory;*" or, "*bury me within fragrant wood.*"

They did not see the carob because they encircled it from above, in that early hour of the afternoon, while a few clouds dissipated on the mountains, and exhausted wolves slept in their burrows. There was no reason to pay attention to that ford in the river, so Yusuf, in order to ease his mind and travel faster, sang softly (to the wonderment of the children, who did not understand him and, with their hands, braided the spider webs among the olive groves in order to have a clear view): "The one who loves you and dies for you, even if he is killed, will return to you." Or, more precisely, one heard:

"*Man youhibbak wa yamout feek,*
hatta law qutil yaoud leek"

Down below, the torrent was flowing, wrapping an arm around the carob, which in that hot hour was folding its branches and closing its leaves all around the mother-son with an abundance of shadows not permeated by the light.

The group continued on, barely catching sight of a small cascade on the river that, swirling, ran over algae and aquatic flowers.

It goes without saying that, inadvertently, they had already left Pino's territory to advance toward the valley and then into the plain being explored by Tirtenio, about whom we had received no news for several days.

Emanuele advised returning to the riverbed and bringing there pieces of cork, leaves, bones and engraved pebbles. In this way the watercourse became a natural refuge for the thoughts of the Arab, who, generally using withered and green leaves all along those uninhabited lands, sent messages that were more easily noticed since they floated atop the waves. Emanuele and Muslim amused themselves by adding bushes and roots, which floated on the river. There was no shortage of bird feathers and empty nests with a mixture of signs and words not always decipherable.

At this point we learned very little about them since Al-Hakim, who was following them, fell asleep on his flying mount and, upon awakening, found himself on the mountains of Le Coste, near Qaltag. He himself was surprised, accusing the lazy sun that diffused an air of torpor and sleep over immense stretches.

We imagined, however, that after having left the banks of the Wadi Hamm and the narrow valley, Yusuf and the children found themselves near Pozzillo. Evening was already descending on Tirtenio's encampment, where some lights lit up Tirtenio's tents, and low, pleasant singing blended with the aroma of cooked food.

Of course they had no suspicion regarding the fate of the woman, nor were they able to gather any news about her, since the few peasants of those areas had been forced to leave and take refuge on the heights.

"Hey you," Muslim would ask when a branch quivered or some noise arose from the territories they had crossed, "have you seen a woman named Aramea?"

Yusuf thought that his wife was heading for the sea to await his arrival, or to call him back from the waves if she were to spot an oblique boat in the distance and smell the scent of ginger or sweet basil.

XVI

The accumulating circumstances showed us that what had happened was nothing more than the result of a wild imagination, that of the men themselves. Nevertheless, my sister, Welly, increased the unknowns. She informed us that our mother, Meliodor, continually chose to be alone in the dark corners of the house or outside on the balcony so as not to disturb anyone, and that she would lose herself at nightfall amid the sounds of the town's one thousand bells.

Moreover, she considered it senseless for us to search for the exact time and position of stellar wheels and to plunge into them with hearts full of emotion. In her opinion, that would take us away from our father's splendor and his uncontaminated journey from the heavens to the earth with inanimate rhythms. To make us understand that she pursued love and not the empty labors of the mind, she left town for the rich valleys and the multitude of nocturnal shadows.

Learning of this, Geber grew worried and, lamenting the time we had lost, went to join her one night, saying to us, "Goodbye, I'm choosing the perfect road."

The news upset us. In fact, his brother Orlando, saddened, took refuge on a plane tree, while Totosimic, hunched over, strolled tirelessly in the moonless night, which brought wafts of fragrant herbs from the ravines and creeks.

With melancholy and hunger, extreme discomfort and visual impairment, we continued along the tortuous roads of the ultramundane blue, with the constant hope of bringing our exploration, conducted far and wide, to a conclusion.

Meanwhile, Welly and Geber, together with the girl, Canopo, were looking for paternal traces in the nocturnal countryside, in the streams of corpuscles and in the swashing coming from the galactic spaces.

They stopped under the trees or in the ruins of abandoned houses and, before interpreting the signs coming from the moon's light and shade, they waited until the birds were sleeping amid the foliage, and the rivers evaporated their exhalations as they had always done.

When Rowley learned of these things, he said that Geber and Welly had been afflicted with narrow-mindedness and had been diverted from celestial ways.

Pino added, "They too have sided with the peasants."

But the two of them, distinguishing each line of the firmament, recorded the vibrations of crystals, spinning electrons and stellar flashes that reached them from above.

They chose the strangest times, when it was possible to capture the shattering of erratic particles in the incommensurable night. These were times when everything was still and the austral wind left darkness in its trail.

Perhaps even the Earth in its obscure journey had an equilibrium of rocks, trees and magnetic bands in that planetary position from which it sent forth, from the opposite side, the shadow of mountains and illuminated oceans to the bottom of very distant wells.

The most sensible of all was Mnemosine, Welly's child, who, with a veil of frost in her hair, followed her mother, at times resting in her arms.

Since she cried without reason and woke up suddenly, the other three realized they had to stop.

And then, the radiations were not like the former ones. That is, there were no murmurs and the uneven striking of granules, but mute transits, tinkling sounds and lazy signals of a center which was a soothing voice and a variety of very sweet sounds. They soon disappeared with hollow echoes and languorous resonances—they were sad, after all—and got lost in ungraspable waves. Then Geber, feeling in his own way united to his departed brother, calmed down and said,

"There's no other course."

As long as we remained in contact with her, Welly would tell us that it was useless to follow crazy illusions and inaccessible paths since there were only spinning galaxies up there that, after midnight, brought back from our father some invisible, voiceless emissions ready to unite with roots, springs and secret golden eggs.

So, I believe, following their nonsense, they no longer saw the light of day. Moreover, they did not leave the borders of Qalat-Minaw's lands, since they thought that fluxes of the night sky would better fall within that circumference, given the almost identical attraction between the memories left by our father and the places natural to him.

"We're all going crazy," shouted Yahin, his eyes red from sleepiness.

Someone managed to see them: dark figures that went from path to path, purposely choosing the most suitable spots. They never stopped—Welly, dressed casually; Canopo, timid and ready to hide at every terrestrial sound so as not to spoil the celestial signals; and Geber, ready to capture such elements in rocky hollows and in gullies, where, according to him, they were concentrated with very pure affluences. Fortunately, the air had become light and was not always perceptible in the moments during which our sister brought small Mnemosine onto the treetops. At those times the rain would stop, the winds would subside, while stellar signals became clearer from precipice to precipice. And if the rotating sidereal entities would happen to be obscured by the clouds and deviated by the frequent hoots of horned owls, Welly, who never tired pursuing the flames of her spirit and the deceptive clues of our father, whom she wanted to join, took from the darkness those rapid looks of love which were usually whispers and dying sounds, and magnified them so that they would propagate on the torrents, on the nocturnal flowers and on the lights of Qalat-Minaw.

Finally, Welly informed us that she would save our mother, Meliodor, whom we had left alone in the large house so that we might follow galactic paths and comets. And there our mother grew sadder and sadder and shriveled up.

Apparently the project stagnated because Welly, trying to pursue whatever appeared more subtle and swift in nature, had put another problem at the center of her preoccupations.

We heard talk of this from a shepherd who visited the camps to resupply them with milk and fresh ricotta.

Yahin, hearing these stories, sighed,

"I'm becoming ridiculous and I'm falling into error."

Welly believed, for example, that even in the dreams of animals and humans some transmissions toward the outside and from the outside to the inside occurred in a thousand ways, and in these oneiric ravelings one could find the purest paternal messages, like seeds reduced to extremely fine undulations.

Our sister, however, constantly wandering at night, would approach hedgehogs, lizards and crickets, and would capture their fleeting images that run through the lands and through the ether in changing wisps of darkness. Canopo, not always satisfied, would follow her, wishing to reach all living species.

Very soon she climbed trees to look for birds. It must not have been an easy task, since at the slightest movement or noise birds awaken and leave the branches. But she found the right angle of incidence to catch the dreams of the feathered ones, and I believe she achieved her goal when the westerly winds made the trees rustle.

She succeeded because of the great number of birds that spring had attracted to the greenery. She looked for sparrows, partridges and jays amid the remaining oak groves; wild doves, robin redbreasts, gold finches, hoopoes and skylarks amid the grassy meadows; and kites and falcons on the rocky terraces.

It was always a matter of imponderable images and a bustle of corpuscles that came from small branches and foliage.

The story became even stranger when it was said that Welly, with Nergal's help, had succeeded in doubling her harvest of those flowing remnants of ions, of changeable aggregates that very rapidly rushed in the nightly circuit of things.

It was said that, during our rests, Nergal joined our sister. His intention was to divide the brains of birds into equal and opposite parts with a laser beam and to draw out double oneiric effects, projections of hundreds and hundreds of dreams, from within to without.

Drop-of-blood smiled when Orlando asked him if what was being said about him was true, and it seemed that with that slight sneer of his he was trying to poke fun at us.

Welly searched for oneiric waves even in the occasional peasants whom she found asleep under leafy boughs, with their heads pointed eastward to take advantage of the sun's first rays.

But we could not continue to follow Geber's and Welly's adventure any further because other events occurred which made us realize that everyone at this point was following his own directive, pursuing Jupiter, Saturn, immense reefs and the evening's solar conjunctions.

XVII

One morning when clouds, harbingers of rain, appeared over Etna after so much good weather, we saw Grandfather Michele coming toward the Castle, with his white hair tousled by Qalat-Minaw's ever-present wind, and with a twig of a flowering acacia in his mouth.

"How nice to see you," he said to us. Then, turning to Mansur, he added, "You're here too?"

Totosimic, Rowley and Atman showed themselves to be upset and, kicking some lindens, accidentally made a number of leaves fall in a blue whirl. To scan the horizon, some old men appeared on the balconies of the houses over whose roofs crowns of orange trees laden with fruit fanned out. Grandfather, with all his majesty, was bringing us neither glory nor benevolence. He shrewdly caught the scent of a distant downpour as he looked at the bent branches of the olive groves in the valley.

"Don't you see that the weather is turning bad?" he said.

And then, "Have you achieved your goal?"

Mansur bowed his head to give him to understand that a great number of problems had arisen, and that it was not clear where they would take us as we went from mirage to mirage. Thinner than before because of his sleepless nights, Grandfather said to us, mincing no words, that acting that way we were not respecting what the deceased man had left behind in the paths of the stars that had enveloped him, and wherever his pensive spirit reigned.

Rowley was puffing smoke from his pipe, Totosimic was scratching the ground with the tip of his shoe, and Orlando, with his fat haggard face, said that no one could replace the advice and friendship that his late brother had offered him in every circumstance.

We went our separate ways so that Grandfather would not be impelled to speak with great excitement as he rearranged and retrieved from his memories peculiar thoughts, impulses, beliefs and shades of ideas that could hinder our progress.

But it was useless. Our silence angered him.

"O Zephir," he cried, turning to me. "You're here too. I didn't expect that. Speaking to you is like speaking to a wall."

A rock losing its balance slid down from the ruins of the Castle. Low clouds hung motionless over Etna's rim.

"What do you expect to find? I've followed you. Who doesn't follow you?" continued the old man, throwing away the blossoming twig. "You are looking for the unknowable. But what clue can you find when everything around you speaks to you of the fluid continuity of things, of solar storms, of birds wandering in the woods, of what is high and of what is low, of what is before the womb and what is after it, of a chaotic mixture of earth, sky, seas, trees and hearts?"

Atman, with his head lowered, was plucking the petals of a white daisy picked under a linden.

"Ah yes," continued Grandfather Michele, touching his ear. "People expect us to make the south wind rise up, and you know very well how everything is subject to change, the comprehensible and the incomprehensible. But the truth escapes your eyes. You are looking for my son's thought, which can still issue from his remains, and from essence to essence and from color to color, like fishermen you throw bait into broad rivers, toward the sun and underground, finding nothing but crazed sea gulls flying over seaweed and dark waves."

Pino clapped one hand against the other, making a wry mouth, until he burst out, "What do you want? What are you saying?"

The old man remained silent with an arm raised halfway in the air. Then, with a gesture indicating great heights, he said that thought is not the moon, nor crystal dust, nor blood, nor cells, nor hollow structure, but the opposite pole of things that in every which way harnesses quartz, calcite, blaring trumpets in a troop of demons, hurricanes and fiery whirlwinds. What is more, one should not consider venous fluxes, summer and winter signs, or very vast stretches of stubble fields that catch fire because of a tiny spark. Becoming increasingly excited, he said that in pursuing the semblances of the deceased, we were moving away from arboreal substance, from the very sad emotions of men, from the generative forces of nature and from the dew that forms on the herbs.

Totosimic asked him why he had come to bother us and, what is more, unannounced, when all sorts of doubts were assailing us, and when his arguments were certainly not such as to shake the tyrannical nature of our kingdom and weaken our belief in all the incorporeal and amorphous things handed down to us by the divinities.

The mass of clouds was slowly rising up the flanks of the mountain. We all remained silent. And Grandfather, undaunted, continued his long-winded speech:

"Link up again uselessly to the perishable igneous atoms that gather together, withdraw and rotate as they cluster in a thousand ways, and go ahead and seek the path of a comet that rises on a fixed date and on a fixed date crosses over to Hades, or the phoenix that comes back to life again in celestial fires, amber and grassy pastures..."

The old man was regaining his strength and ardor, so we left him. Some went toward the cliff of the Castle; others toward the slope of the town, where the women were shutting their windows and balconies; and still others toward the heaps of rocks green with ivy; but all of us, from different locations, heard these arbitrary, ringing and bewildering words: "*osi, osi, ioni, sososo, ule, ujleuleule, gasgasgas, terra, erra, erra, ite, predire, predire, ire, ire, sapermife, iocchi, iocchi, s...ssss...*"

Speaking now only to the stones, the clay and the white windows of Qalat-Minaw, Grandfather Michele smiled, wrinkling his nose, and motioned us to leave and to credulously pursue natural changes. Then, still smiling, and accompanied by Mansur, with a slow gait he headed for his house, a side of which faced the square in front of the temple.

He did not leave us serene. Gathering together we felt we had witnessed a dubious structure of wondrous but senseless apparitions, of eccentric orbits of Mercury, of cycles and epicycles in the midst of a desolate countryside.

Totosimic told us bluntly that he would leave us not so much because of what the old man had told us but because he himself believed that Nife, or the center of the earth, was the source from which everything springs: white and red rocks, rivers, ponds and fluid vapors that shook the earth's crust and, splitting it, produced extremely loud rumbles. It was there that one had to seek the paternal traces, which could be found neither increased nor diminished but in their pristine purity. And of this we could be certain if we kept in mind that for days and days we had been following the whims of alchemists and astronomers who had never been seen, and who prompted us to navigate senselessly through starry archipelagos.

We were taken by surprise, and each of us looked at Atman, who sat impassibly on a pepper tree, crushing its small fruit and pointing to the arc of the sky that was closing over the Ionian Sea and the Ereian Mountains. Then Al-Hakim told us that the scholars worked at night, and that nothing is visible in the darkness. He also said that one should not be concerned if up till now they had not appeared to us, since many clues confirmed their actual existence. For example, once Mansur had seen four or five of them on top of our house, and they were hardly visible because of the trailing mist of that hour. They were engaged in heated discussions concerning mechanical questions, and since their attention was focused on the heavens and on stellar diagrams, they concentrated on the effects of Jupiter, Uranus and Pluto, jumping from roof to roof, over the chimneys and dividing walls of the houses. Some peasants said that they too had seen them, but not very clearly because of the nocturnal fluxes. The scholars were dressed in strange clothes and had very white beards on which the lights of the firmament concentrated their rays by the thousands. Albumasar, the king of kings, was probably the tallest, or at least that's how he appeared because of a deformation caused by stellar irradiations. His shadow slithered easily in opposite directions, from roof to roof and from eaves to eaves.

It was not easy to look at him because mouths, tongues and eyes remained still and stupified seeing him employ occult means to shoo away bats, sounds and thin vapors. And down from Albumasar, in open channels, starry light shone on the cold surface of the lands or on the mountain tops, and always at night.

Al-Hakim added that sometimes when Cheràstrata had trouble falling asleep, she leaned up against a wall, as was her custom, and had seen the scholars preceded by Albusmasar, while behind them ever-swarthy Jafar collected dewdrops and sprinkled great quantities of light elements around him.

At this point Aunt Agrippa said that those were sublunar traces of our deceased father which the wind very quickly turned into dust and sudden flashes in the air.

Rowley said,

"Al-Hakim, you are mistaking the humors of clouds and their bolts for what is seething in your spirit."

Orlando, lost in thought, objected,

"I wouldn't say that."

Atman was quiet and seemed to expand the pepper tree, moving about within it and spreading the branches apart with his arms.

According to Al-Hakim, there were even some old men who posted themselves in the hollow walls of the houses in order to spot those wizards at night. Behind Jafar they had seen Eddington, who walked on the roofs with his dazzling locks in the air that the nebulae out in space projected on Qalat-Minaw, or who with one hand pulverized the falling stars that, being more numerous because of the milder season, lit up the firmament like tiny sickles, as white as lambskins. It was necessary to squint one's eyes to see them.

The last to come was bald Hubble. Though he was the shortest of them all, he managed all the same to put out, from distances of a thousand arms, the candles lit in the towers and the street lamps, especially when Mars was close to Earth. And then the town, without lights, rose up toward the stellar circles, multiplying the sparkles of crystalline stones and fissile flints.

"O Al-Hakim, what are you saying?" cut in Uncle Pino.

"In my opinion," said the Arab, "it was the scholars and Aunt Agrippa who reanimated Aramea's graft by piercing it with rays that are giving it new life and that are gradually allowing the buds and the vegetation to grow."

Totosimic interrupted him, telling us that there was no escape now since the reasons for our disagreement had multiplied tenfold, and that it was useless to continue together when one did not know what one wanted, and the opposing theses and bits of evidence had led us astray. That is why he wanted to leave us and pursue his destiny, which he considered to be the best possible.

We looked toward the flanks of Qalat-Minaw where the lamps had been extinguished, and everything looked like a large black blotch, except for the lights of the towns which clambered up the slopes of Etna. And Atman, climbing down from the tree, said,

"Up there is where we've got to find his remains—in the heavens; everyone says so, even the birds of the night."

But Totosimic answered, no, no, and rising, he specified that the position of earthly things taken from right to left could not send us back the paternal effluences. He also said that he could not follow us in our peregrination, since springs, subterranean rocks and boiling magma were leading him, from cliff to cliff, following sane logic, to the forges of Nife.

So, he left us that same day, descending toward the Washhouse and telling us that he would be joining Geber and Welly.

XVIII

Three of our relatives had left us: Tirtenio, Geber and Totosimic. The rest of us were still rather willing to continue the explorations, but Orlando advised us to gather information about his three brothers, seeing that the respective groups had left their huts and tents and had gone to unknown regions. Bethsam, agreeing with him, said:

"We still have to keep in contact with one another."

But the problem could not have easily been solved if Orlando, smiling affably, had not told us that one of his childhood friends could help us; namely, Muhallhel, who, being the caretaker of the cemetery, was rarely seen in town.

"Oh, that's a good one!" exclaimed Rowley. "What can he tell us?"

Pino was against the idea because he had no faith in Muhallhel, whom he had occasionally heard talk of as a man no one managed to see, much less meet.

"Orlando," he said, "do you want us to lose track of Tirtenio and Geber?"

So it ended there. The days passed without any reliable news reaching us from our dear relatives, and all we could do, in the diaphanous air, was gaze at the blueness dying out in the dark gorges.

"Come on," said Bethsam. "What'll it cost us to meet with Muhallhel? If he's there, he's there; if he's not, he's not."

So we headed for the cemetery, Orlando, Rowley, Mansur and I, with Nergal following us, though reluctantly. It was a place that received consistency and color from the underlying plains and the winding fields nearby, where grain grew sluggishly. According to Orlando, Muhallhel was a guest of the Capuchins whose monastery rose up at the entrance of that dismal place. And, according to Father Benedetto, who welcomed us, the man, timid and bizarre as he was, could not be found easily. He would go from corridor to corridor and from cell to cell, often to sit high up in the bell tower, which continually told the time with the tolling of bells used by the peasants scattered about the countryside to regulate their work in the fields.

In the meantime, old Father Benedetto showed us a library with millions of books in the corridors, staircases and even under the eaves. Here was stored a work that had taken years to complete and that regarded the fate of every inhabitant of Qalat-Minaw. Here and there, hidden among jugs, small tear bottles, scimitars, gorgets and gunstocks, were manuscripts dealing with our adventure.

"Who could have expected such a result?" thought Rowley worriedly, as he lit his pipe to avoid smelling the musty odor of the room and the saltpeter.

On Orlando's advice, we went outside in the hope of meeting his friend in one of the paths of the graveyard. We saw a small man run toward some clumps of sunflowers. When the man recognized Orlando's voice, he stopped and asked him,

"Why have you come here with so many men?"

Orlando ran up to him and embraced him, telling him that we needed his help in finding out what had become of Tirtenio, Geber and Welly. Muhallhel had a leathery face partially covered by the visor of his cap.

"Good morning," he said. "No one comes to these parts if not invited."

Mansur exclaimed,

"I've seen you before."

Muhallhel explained that he did not leave that place because everything was there. Death, he said, is not the privation of light (because privation is nothing, whereas mortal darkness is the opposite of light); it is an amplification of lights and shadows in materials of that very large animal that is our earth, whose consciousness exists in rocks, in the bones of the dead, in trees and down below, in hot metals.

Rowley scratched his blond beard. Mansur smiled. The small man told us that by means of bird sounds and changing patterns of air and earth tremors, he was collecting graphs indicating the fate of Tirtenio and Totosimic, about whom, for the time being, he could tell us nothing precisely.

So, seeing him every Monday and Friday afternoon, we managed to make him less suspicious and to gain additional knowledge concerning the secrets of his heart.

We learned much from Orlando, who secretly led us down small paths into grottos and areas of grassy scrub. The cemetery was not large, after all, if you consider that, besides a central section, it had only two lateral sections: one exposed to the eastern and southern winds, the other to the western wind.

Perpetual breezes came from the equinoctial band and, depending on whether it was autumn or spring, brought moisture or steam that rose toward the mountains of Qalat-Minaw, where the latter flung them back to the four main points of the earth. Muhallhel, marking the ground with furrows, had depicted twelve winds, and among these grooves he depicted others, such as the zephyrs and breezes that shake the stems of herbs and flowers in April and carry pollen in yellow-blue currents to the hill of the cemetery.

But the work he did not speak of, if not by allusion, was something else. He classified the dead: he opened their eyes, examined their foreheads and, breathing in their ultimate odors, decided, never erring, whether to bury them in the southern or northern section of the cemetery. In so doing, he believed he was dealing with sublime matters.

He gave us to understand that it was almost always a case of common folk who had died and had no reason to live. Muhallhel would dissolve them in the terrestrial pits and occult sands of the mountain, and would channel the resultant heavy, clotted waters and filthy elements among the brambles and fertile lands of the valley on our right.

When Uncle Pino came to see us against his better judgement, he ruffled his white hair as he heard such stories, and told us in a whisper that it was time to go and to leave these places where stones were corroded by acrimony and drops were crystallizing into dew.

In the section on the left, Muhallhel buried people in whose white eyes and hair he did not find diriment signs, and simply from certain declivous swellings, from late intestinal rumblings and from their scrotums hanging like bladders, he understood that they were devoid of excellent traits, such as in the case of weaklings, nitwits, philistines, bigots, panderers and so forth.

From the embankment grew thalluses, shrubs and curious trees, all sharing a metallic-vegetal nature. The roots below clung to the bones, which were transformed into the substance of a tree, without any intermediary seed. This was accomplished by means of small subterranean flames and the smoke of will-o'-the-wisps that at night clung to rows of red stones called cinnabar. So, with the help of rainwater, and sulfureous and other mineral waters that the bodies produced, there came into being, from the foregoing slope, pieces of wood without veins or branches. They were always at ground level, lying in a pile of tree trunks lacking wooden spirals and sap-carrying veins. In brief, it was a mockery of arboreal figures serpentining in a thousand ways on clods and stony nodes, and sucking nutriment from the decomposing bodies or from the earth itself. All one had to do was to scratch their surface to see not only their mass reduced, naturally, but also their mineral-wooden density. What is more, dark beige was the predominant color, and no buds were seen, except for certain whitish spots at the edges, but in themselves they were empty and floury. In a word, they were specks of dirt. And even when burned, the wood preserved its glowing embers for a long time, its fuel being consumed very slowly. And it released foul-smelling smoke that made the peasants living in the ravines shut the doors of their hovels and say,

"What's Muhallhel doing up there?"

The man gave little importance to these essentially barren fields that no one had claimed because of their foul smells. But going there during a fiery dusk, as Rowley, Atman, Nergal and I happened to do, we saw that it was not easy to detect whether it was old burnt wood or petrified tree trunks that looked like hard rocks. Nergal, interested in everything we found, spooned out some of the outer layer and said that the inner one was composed of living wood, or vice versa.

Because of the tumultuous growth of so many trees, a great number of them fell with thuds into the ditches below and into quagmires where lifeless water stagnated. And there, pieces of bark, chunks of clay, crinkled wisps of oval and dentate leaves seethed, obviously lifeless, but similar to mushroom-beds of wood and stones.

"Come on," said Uncle Pino when he saw the ditches. "What devil brought us here?"

He scolded his brother Orlando, saying to him,

"I didn't know of these tastes of yours!"

But the level ground of the cemetery, that is, the central section, was reserved for the chosen ones, that is, for the remains of those whom Muhallhel considered suitable because of their wondrous fertilizing properties. It was not easy to be admitted there, because the caretaker studied them when there was a new moon and infinite atoms fell from the heavens in multiple rays and, bound and clustered, thrust back toward the center of the earth what was opaque and heavy, while those whirls of atoms and the stars turned into innumerable glimmers, sending forth a multitude of scents.

Muhallhel identified the bodies of the most sensitive, of the ardent, of the most intelligent, and not seen by anyone, he calmly exposed them to the nocturnal air to proceed later to their interment.

That spot differed from the other two sections because of its light colors and the lush growth of its green plots. There, utricular or testicular grass, repugnant in smell, did not grow; but sunflowers and petunias, growing continuously taller with the rising of the sun, turned from east to west—gradually, of course—and cypresses, laurel trees and the few palms turned their treetops westward to take advantage of the blowing summer winds.

That wasn't all, because, down there, bushes, snapdragons, borage plants and gillyflowers followed the lateral movement of the sun, day after day.

Muhallhel spoke to us of solar herbs and lunar herbs, the former, brighter and bluish in color; the latter, tremulous and with silvery buds like heather, for example, or mosses. The former were in the furrows on the right; the latter in those on the left. As they flourished, they exchanged pollen, heliotrope with heliotrope; leaves, olive with olive; roots, vervain with vervain. And among them there were agreements, passions and daily and nightly chimeras.

Muhallhel further differentiated between male and female trees. He showed us some slim cypresses with flexible tops that bent toward other cypresses rich in berries and wooden barbs, and he said that they were in love, being of the opposite sex. Some trees, for example, became sad because they were alone; and griefstricken, arched and avoided the winds, twisting their large and small branches without casting shadows.

Yahin observed,

"It's a fertile land. It could yield bushels of wheat."

In a spot on the terrace, neither myrtles nor laurels nor junipers grew, but a very soft grass already dry when it sprouted, and around it there was gravelly earth. Yahin asked, "How come?"

The little man made a grimace, not one of disgust but of sorrow, and gave us to understand, with many gestures, that his wife was buried there. So as not to upset him, Orlando told us in a whisper that she had been a woman-hen and had spoken to Muhallhel only of money and menses, and dazing him, had prevented him from concluding any thought. That is why he had chosen this job as caretaker.

Uncle Pino scratched his head and looked around. Though we were in the month of May, he did not see anything other than small barren trees and vines that tried to grasp and hug each other on the ground, clinging by their tips and fixing themselves in the ground in order to generate new roots and proliferate. And so he asked why this could happen. But the caretaker changed the subject and spoke to us of his two (or three? He could not recall anymore) sons who had gone to Greenland to ask the multitude of seals and penguins that adorned the frozen deserts with black, for peace and love.

Nergal smiled, not regarding his sons, of course—poor souls—but because of that section of the cemetery where the chosen spirits lay. Pointing his thumb repeatedly downward, he observed that because of the scarcity of bodies that month, very few heat vapors and will-o'-the-wisps were meandering underground, and this could be seen from the small amount of sulfureous smoke that rose from the fissures in the clods.

"Now, what does that have to do with anything?" asked Rowley.

Muhallhel blushed and with an excuse went off among the low clay tombs. Then Nergal joyfully shouted,

"But don't you understand that these trees are sterile? And don't you understand that this place abounds in trees and plants in the winter?"

Pino:

"Why?"

Bethsam:

"What in the world are you saying?"

Nergal, feeling more confident, pointed out that the true vegetal-animal trees were ours, those that in the future we would grow on the hills and in the forests. They would be palpitating with a spirit and with senses. They would not be like these that rose up around us in a confusion of nerves, small veins, wooden parts and almost flesh-colored azaroles. The trees around us, squalid males and sad females with thick bark and on the whole black, turned mostly eastward and did not have vital seeds, but grew directly and proportionately from the cadavers below, being sterile shoots of the same. Their trunks were not solid, and their boughs were not white or lustrous. They enclosed petrified crystalline humors, black burned material of people who no longer experienced the great expanse of sky, swimming celestial irradiations and the incommensurable course of photons. They were trees with roots springing from mouths, hearts, brains, ears and bones. And they filled that section of the cemetery with false, ephemeral colors, making nitrous waters flow. Their fibers, up above, multiplied unequally in the alternating petals of sterile flowers of an indefinite nature with stunted, odorless stems: flowers aptly called "melancholics," which did not open in the bright sun but only in the middle of the night when nothing is heard. And they were overcome by dawn, which, in making them sadder, caused them to shut, bend their stems and fall on the sandy soil.

Since Muhallhel never returned, Nergal continued to defend his thesis. He spoke to us of cadaverous juices that retreated in the roots in the winter, swelling and sealing the pores, and in the spring, with the fermentation of nitrous salts, rose again from the scanty remains of the few cadavers mentioned above, through the bark to the extreme branches of the treetops, bursting out, no longer restrained by the cold, into leaves and buds. Obviously they were ephemeral, being immediately consumed by the continuous conversion of the dead's remains into nourishment. And this did not occur in the countryside of Qalat-Minaw, where boughs and small branches took from the sun and the dense earth the vital juices that permeated the arboreal meatuses and pores because of their natural viscosity. He also tried to talk to us of Aramea and her limbs, which were joined in a continuous ascent to the fibers and plexuses of her son's sentiment, but Orlando interrupted him: "Let's return to the monastery. Muhallhel will grieve all day long because we have discovered the bleak origin of his trees. Who knows what he might be thinking. It's Tirtenio's and Totosimic's fate that concerns us."

We returned to the old building. Since we opened the door carefully, the little bell did not ring, and one at a time we entered, unseen.

By searching here and there, we discovered, scattered in jugs, within holes and in the hollow spaces of the nests that swallows had built under the roof tiles, a curious "Fragmenta Tirtenii," which Muhallhel had composed in the form of passages, suras and prayers mixed with personal observations and ultramundane "paternal" searches. It had a profusion of notes and glosses at the foot of each page, but from it all we could not infer the destiny of Tirtenio. Invoking himself on the first page as a man who wished to enliven a place of the dead with purifying waters and to renovate it with greenery and serene spirits, Muhallhel wrote that excerpts of that journal had been found on the shore between Càtana and Corinth, amid the gravel and the remains of jellyfish. It was not easy for us to decipher it, but, thank goodness, Al-Hakim helped us, reading the most muddled pages from back to front.

XIX

Anyway, thanks to that manuscript, we were able to determine that on the 18th of April (a month after our father's demise), Tirtenio and his group had left the campsite at Pozzillo, a rather damp area where already before nightfall mist moved from plant to plant, depositing heavy dew that moistened the clover and the few artichoke fields below.

Meanwhile Yusuf, unable to find any other road, happened to join us and was not well-accepted by everybody, especially not by Tirtenio, who felt irritated by the Arab's presence. Yusuf was unaware of the grafting of Aramea and Diofar, and so he persisted obstinately in looking for her to the detriment of our enterprise that changes and confusion had brought to the brink of error. The first days, when we were still camping at Pozzillo, Muslim, Emanuele, Ziritia and the others amused themselves by hunting lizards, which they hung with strands of barley on trees, rendering the branches rich in reflections and cooling them down from the heat that enveloped them toward noon. Cooling, in that way, the air nearby and filling the trees with boughs, the shade lingered in the timber and reached down to the tired men.

Many looked toward the Ionian Sea, which was not visible from the plain, and climbed the olive trees and the few quinces in order to feel the briny vapors that formed in the afternoon. Many, indirectly prompted by Tirtenio, wanted to leave the thick roots and the land of Qalat-Minaw to head through mud and torrents toward the kingdoms of the sea, and finally to sit on the shore, carefree and mindless, in the breeze and gusts of the Auster. But Tirtenio, bound to us because of his love for the one who had left us, decided to leave the reddish plains of poppies, and the utricles and mosses of the thickets, in order to broaden his search in the sea. Strangely, he found himself in accord with Yusuf, who believed that his wife and his son, craving infinite waters, had become lost in the Ionian Sea, having left the land that, during the day, sent shade and heat aloft, and at night, filling the air with brine, froze the humors of buds.

"So be it!" they shouted in chorus when Tirtenio suggested that they all go to the sea. The children said that they would not leave those areas and, making a pile of serpents, wasps and leafy branches, set it on fire to celebrate the group's departure. When the group was far away, they waved goodbye to it from an oak tree, having fun hearing their echo, which suddenly returned from Palica.

"Goodbye, Yusuf," they said.

And Yusuf said:

"Follow me. Leave these mountains."

And they:

"Goodbye, Yusuf."

Ziritia and Mariela, weeping, said to him,

"Leave us at least a bottle full of clouds."

"Let's take the paved road," Tirtenio said. But Yusuf advised against that, saying that they had better keep pure for the great enterprise and, therefore, avoid the inhabited lands and roads of the island, which were traversed night and day by cars and shouting men.

They took another road, heading for Corinth, proceeding amid numerous orange groves whose remaining fruits, heavy and ripe, fell to the ground at the slightest sound and were soon enveloped by the reflections of very low stars, the slime of snails and the tufts below. They traveled in the darkness so as not to be seen, and to avoid the daily contaminations of men and the strong scent of herbs.

Yusuf guided himself by looking at the Ursa Major, which shone directly over his head and reverberated on the tangerine trees, the stones and the drops of water dispersed in the air. Several women followed them, among whom was Zyiàd, who had left her old father under the mountains of Arcura because he had allied himself decisively with the peasants.

The first part of the voyage was pleasant, and they sang in deserted areas to encourage one another or picked oranges in large orchards to quench their thirst.

From the twelfth, fifteenth and twenty-first fragments of the above-mentioned "small treatise," it seemed that, during the first days, Zyiàd, though a very mature girl, was lonesome for the countryside she had left. That was a place where the clods softened by the recent diluvial rains had abounded in scents of pomegranate blossoms, growing mint, and indigenous seeds sprouting in ditches. In a word, she missed the soothing ebb and flow that could not be felt in the plain.

It took them three days to reach the sea, continually crossing deserted lands along the Ibleian mountain range, whose slopes and limestone tuff had already been invaded by bees, and where narcissus, sage and poppies bloomed. That is why they traveled even during the final hours of the day. Yusuf, before nightfall, climbed a eucalyptus tree and from up there examined the countryside in order to select the best routes. He stayed there for quite a while, crouched on the branches. And since the men still could not see the Ionian Sea, many of them began to murmur—despite the fact that Tirtenio tried to restrain them. They contended that they had been tricked concerning the length of the journey. Yusuf, from the eucalyptus tree, said,

"What are you afraid of, you wretched men? Before long the sun will set and night will be upon us. We'll rest and then continue our journey."

Meanwhile, he tarried on the tree he had chosen, his face turned toward the sunset. He was waiting for the rising (and sometimes the setting) of the stars, and the imminent arrival of the etesian winds. These winds were to bring peace to the sulking men, who were lighting fires to prepare their meal.

Yusuf spent several hours on eucalyptus trees and holm oaks to see the rising of the constellations of the Dog, Arcturus and the Pleiades, and to follow their serene movements in the celestial arc. And from the smells of the waters he was determining their direction and the quality of the springs from which they came. To amuse his companions, he spoke of hidden passageways through which spring waters flow. Some of the waters, which are heavy and rich in brine, gush forth from terrestrial openings, run through fertile fields and encrust roots with salts. Others are sweet and limpid, being purged of sand and colloids, and flow in canals and streams, through clay stretches and hot lands, to the sea. And still others, which are black and muddy, come from the mountains and are trapped in underground passages and, for the most part, in ditches.

And down below they all listened to him.

A few days later, at dawn, they saw the sea, a stretch of air and waves moved by the eastern winds. Some shouted,

"Here's the goal of our dreams!"

And others,

"Let there be light!"

No one could be seen except a fisherman who had already set out to sea and with consecutive strokes gave the proper impetus to the oars. Corinth, drenched in sunlight, was in the distance to their right. But the men did not wish to undertake the adventure immediately, and Tirtenio, too, preferred having his men get used to the absence of rain clouds, hills and animals. Yusuf was happy—one could say he was overjoyed—and he kissed the foaming waves that died out on the sandy shore. And in order to avoid speaking of Aramea and their child, and expressing his sentiments publicly like that, he said to his companions that the sea lives and moves, obviously not as they do but in a circle that brings it from east to west. Its swirling waters become rarefied and swell, rising in straits and covering the four corners of the earth because it is attracted by the orbiting sun and the nocturnal moon.

The men listened. Aristarco, the eldest, asked,

"When all is said and done, it would have been better to stay in Qalat-Minaw, don't you all agree?"

But Yusuf continued his discourse in order to dissipate the doubts in the others.

He said that solar fires render the waters of the oceans light, making vapors and dust escape, while farther ahead, always in the same latitude, waves swell and grow, but at the passage of the sun they boil a little and sink, and the resultant depressions occur over great distances according to the birth and death of the day.

Yusuf was a good speaker. That is why Tirtenio began to respect him, even if he did not reveal to him our past secrets and what we were hoping to achieve amid the waters. Sitting on the beach, he cooled his feet in the surf and looked into the distance, shielding his eyes with his white forelock.

Yusuf, our Arab relative, spoke further of waterspouts rising perpendicularly to the sun, and of globular waves rising up behind and in front; and not only that, but also of the daily activity of the oceans that rise and fall along the sides of the earth, creating trenches and abysses abounding in fish. And the sea, like men, knows no peace, its paths continually opposed by tides and occasional conches. What is more, at night, it is swollen by warm lunar rays and the bustle of large, sleepless fish.

But the group was not happy, even though it had already reached the shore of the yearned for Ionian Sea. And the men, one at a time, and then in twos and threes, etc., were stricken with burning fevers, the darkening of their urine, insomnia and diarrhea. The illness was rampant, despite the belladonna leaves and flowers, and the poppy powder that Yusuf administered. Maximum caution in the selection of the food was not enough, because extreme fatigue persisted in the weakened bodies. Everyone dreamed of returning to the heights, but Tirtenio found that absurd; and so did our Arabic relative, who, keeping watch during the night, privately asked the low marina, the mustard hedges and the kelp if they had heard the soft cries of a woman or a mermaid in the scattered blackness of the sea, or the faint weeping of dying corals clinging to a small child.

Efforts and care were redoubled, but the diarrhea, alternating with intermittent fever, continued, and the various sorts of intestinal tonics were insufficient, including theriaca and black poppy seeds. I cannot add anything else because, at this point, one would need the pen of a wizard or that of a doctor.

Among other things, the members of the squad had no interest in the future, and they were prey to all sorts of bodily illnesses; they were absentminded and distracted, with their minds fixed on the sea gulls, high in the air, that enchanted them with their flights. Tirtenio realized that the distance from Qalat-Minaw, from its zephyrs and valley grass, had sapped the spirits of his men. Thank goodness that, besides Zyiàd, there were three young women with them who collected everlastings and reeds from the nearby fields. With these, they changed the direction of the morning breezes, sending them in the direction of their companions, thus helping them endure their sufferings. Many called them, even from their tents,

"Al Zerzour!"

"Al Aas!"

"Al Zajal!"

And at times of greater discomfort they called them:

"*Al dorrat al thamina!*" which means "precious pearl."

Al Zajal was the most silent of the three, and beside spreading pollen around by blowing on the everlastings, she prepared potions of cubeb, ginger, she-donkey milk and cinnamon bark for everybody. And also of cardamom. Al Ass smeared lilac balsam and unguent from Mecca on those who were feverish, adding mustard seeds to make the applications more vigorous. To avoid being looked at in the face, and thus generate turmoil in the innumerable canals of the men and weaken them all the more, the women, before every task, put on melhafa veils, of which they had a good supply.

Once the circulation of the bile was improved and the abundance of excretory humors diminished, the group recovered from their fevers when Orion appeared—the celestial sword that slowly rose from the horizon. The violent headaches that had afflicted more than ten men vanished. The three women were of considerable help in their recovery. To get the men used to the uniform surface of the sea, they pointed to the swallows that flew about near the coast, and to the kingfishers, high in the air, that flapped amid the exhalations of water.

The day set for the departure arrived. Perhaps because of the turmoil, or the fever that Yusuf probably got, the journal contains very little more than allusions and insignificant lines traced with a weak hand.

I believe that Tirtenio left our island unexpectedly to keep his men from thinking about the fires lit on the mountains of Qamut, and about the olive groves.

The three girls sang, accompanying Zyiàd, who was thinking of her old father and pomegranate blossoms, while the sea swelled and became greener, its transparent waters revealing violet rocks and tufts of seaweed. I presume it was not a happy moment for anyone, because, leaving the familiar face of the land, they were confronting wandering starfish, abysses, urticarial sea anemones and whatever beneath them was unknown.

Yusuf spoke to his companions, who were huddled in fear. He said that frost, ice, springs and the sea are made of material that breathes and feels. The radiations filtered by the atmosphere, and the sea winds in the morning, spread from wave to wave, making everything white. At noon, they make the Ionian Sea, the Mediterranean Sea and the oceans blue. He also said that they raise yellow regurgitations of ferrous sediments from the depths to the surface. And in the afternoon, in opaque stains they intersect the diaphanous red that spreads over the waters, from mountain to mountain and from shore to shore.

Meanwhile, night fell, turning them into what looked like aquatic creatures visible only to sea fans, corals and distant reefs.

During the first days, the squad was beset with regrets and uncertainties since the men had divergent opinions and they were constantly tormented by their memory of Qalat-Minaw.

Old Aristarco, for example, proposed that they follow the currents that, like wide rivers with their own banks, cross the sea with fury, making a great deal of noise and avoiding one another; what is more, they rise and fall over hundreds of miles when the northeast wind blows; on steep banks at the bottom of the sea, they uncover grottos, stalactites and, farther up, madrepores, sponges and sargasso mixed with copper and silver dust. There, said Aristarco, one could look at one's image, speak to oneself and hear the echoes of our father's voice, which grew pleasantly louder with the appearance of the constellations, and with the disappearance of the same, languished and vanished in marine meanders.

Others were confused by the flow of the Ionian Sea, which advanced from east to southeast, rolling and unrolling in endless breakers. They felt an extremely strong yearning for an unreachable past comprised of cock crowings, ruffled nettles, oil lamps and ditches full of scabiosa and periwinkles.

"Hey, what's wrong with you?" shouted Tirtenio.

They could not help feeling they were still at the beginning of an adventure that had transformed them into pilgrims of love.

To encourage them, Tirtenio made them keep their eyes fixed on the sparse blue-green flowers and on patches of foam, and at night he lit up the mouths of the rivers by burning cattails, and he directed their eyes to the supermundane signs of the zodiac. To distract their attention from the surface of the waters, he, assisted by the young women, persuaded them to rest their faces on the waves to get them used to the idea of identifying with pearls, pale starfish and, down below, with emeralds, topazes and reefs of black stone. So, gradually, they no longer thought of bees that spring off the backs of oxen or of flowering broomrape that grows in broad bean fields. They turned their minds and hearts more and more to the sea abysses and to the rocks erupting interminably in shapes of different material.

It was an unusual adventure. By then they were far from personal objectives, having different properties, for they occupied tiny spaces in the immense quantity of water.

Having left a familiar world, they felt they were no longer the same but diversified in another reality. Looking up from the depths of the sea, they did not see one sunset hour but a thousand of them broken up into so many colors. They no longer saw one face of the companion beside them but a thousand of them distorted by random rays. There was not one star, that most finely struck them in the eyes, but many stars all around, and these were lost in quivering showers of light and in sprays that that late hour turned purplish and violet.

Some of the men silently asked themselves what was happening to them, being rejoined and immediately flung into curls of waves (very light waves unconnected to the others), and slowly dragged by the refluxes of dark currents. They saw the pale and dismal whiteness of the day filtering in the whirlpools, and the afternoon lengthened by the retreating sun, which was dying out with blood-red vapors on the breakers. And at night they did not perceive the wind nor the Milky Way, but the absence of light, shadows that multiplied and shadows that clustered on the seaweed. In that world, Tirtineo hoped to find the fleeting traces of the departed one, to decipher them and, from place to place, collect their essences together with the sluggish attacks of the thanatobird.

So, having left the Ionian Sea, they crossed immense stretches of water, reemerging amid skeletons of fish, amethysts, unrecognizable bones and, farther on, amid dripping gem dust, fins, plankton, clusters of red eggs and small conches blowing in the waves.

During the night they made use of the vestiges of Mars, Saturn and Jupiter to guide them through passageways and winding paths, and to allow them to penetrate into the smallest streams of water that extended to valleys and grottos.

From the "Fragmenta Tirtenii" we learned that their presence was noted in the Mediterranean Sea and along the terrestrial arcs upon which oceans travel. I believe that they were at the limit of the visible, on the edges of abysses from which terrestrial humors emerged in bands, coalesced and finally disappeared in the deepest spots.

By then they no longer felt the desire to return to land, having lost their memory of green hills, the clay gullies of Qalat-Minaw and the ephemeral blooming of flowers. They went from abyss to abyss, with the daily movements of the heavens having no meaning for them.

The most lighthearted were the girls: white figures that adorned themselves with lapis lazzuli, salt crystals and sea gems that made their eyes seem very long. They readily showed their feelings when at dusk they were seized by a desire for the mountains of Arcura and for olive trees, as happened to Zyiàd. Then the tremulous waters became more opaque around this woman, their scattered blotches vibrating dolefully on the scales of dead fish.

It took a long time for Tirtenio to realize that he had entered another path, where one would not find traces of our father except in the form of unusual black herbs and changing vortexes. He thought that by navigating in different latitudes, he could draw up a map of the route taken by the semblances of the departed one.

Nor could he count on Yusuf's help, for the latter, as you can easily understand, was concentrating on fields of closed flowers that changed appearance according to the time of day, and on the mouths of rivers, along the coasts, that carried gold dust, swollen leaves and fish eggs from high areas.

They never again returned to land. Between themselves and the past they interposed underwater mountains, sea trees and heaths of seaweed filtering distant nebulae.

Tirtenio still believed that our terrestrial perspectives were misleading, finding in the sea the natural principle that could contain and dissolve the lost essences in so many areas. So, on and on he went, followed by the others, except Yusuf and Zyiàd, who were now shapeless bodies mixed with clouds of fish and dying glimmers that came from above. They had become sand, waves and pale green seaweed. They felt reintegrated in a primordial unity. Yet they had the slim possibility of absorbing inviolate rays of light, magnesium, iron, darkness and the sounds of very small trumpets that in themselves were empty and infinite.

Nor do I believe that they were able to communicate with one another any longer, if not through variations in temperature, sound, growth, the flowering of marine plants and desires that sadly vibrated in the underwater caves. This was what was happening particularly to Yusuf and to Zyiàd, who, having left the group, tried to rise up over the submarine seascapes through paths of brine and remnants of old stubble and of lunar dehiscences. The young man was already communicating with the fish about his worries and thoughts, and he asked them and the regularly moving tides about Diofar and Aramea. Of course, no one could answer. But intensifying the light of his heart, he continually asked the caverns of

Tartarean stone, the wriggling swordfish and the perforated cliffs of the abysses about Diofar. Of course, no one answered. Imprisoned in the obsession of his desires, he knocked on the walls of the king of the sea's castle; he lamented from the heights of the grottos; and he played the great harp of the marine reeds to be heard better. It seems that he rested in a niche with Zyiàd at his side, distressed that the hundredfold multiplication of the sounds he made received no answer. Then they withdrew, leaving one another. They curled up and cursed the sullen eye of the ocean.

Some news reached us from fishermen or indirectly from migrating swallows and the leaves of marine privet torn away by the wind.

But they were legends that for us, who had remained on the heights of the Castle, were images and the distorted rhythms of streams of atoms that came from the firmament and sank inexplicably into the sea.

Solitary fishermen lost in their very long journeys felt expanding from below, in nights of the new moon, broken and lifeless voices in different timbres. One was gloomier; it spoke of air, fire, water and of nothing, and was perpetually directed from breaker to breaker toward the Ionian Sea. The other was sweeter and feminine, and reemerged atop the waves with the longings of love.

These songs were heard all around the world: near the twin seas, along the African coasts, in remote Chile and on the frigid ice packs of the poles. It seems that whales ceased traveling and people on the shores looked for mermaids. The water slowly brought that faint mixture of sounds to the juniper trees and the plume grass, and into the mouths of the estuaries. And these sounds, which were always doleful, emerged from the dark meatuses of the land through springs. Sailors related that they suddenly heard these words in the seething waves:

"Lau qadar qalbi yansak,
lam youalef al oghnia dhi."

Al-Hakim, smiling at the importance we gave those accounts, told us that the words mean: "If my heart could leave you, it would not compose this song." Yahin added that we had better not lose time like children listening to meaningless fables, while the wheat left in the fields by the fugitive peasants was ripening and begging to be cut down. In reality, during the first days, Pino, Orlando, Mansur and I followed the clouds that arose from the sea, but then we no longer paid attention to the rumors concerning those who had disappeared. And when someone spoke of Yusuf and of Zyiàd, we kept silent, looking in the direction of the Wadi Hamm.

XX

We were convinced that we had lost the path of our father's illusory destiny—not just strayed from it. So, at that point, we would have wasted our days lying on the grass of the heights, if Atman, Salvat and Rowley had not insistently spurred us on to resume our celestial excursions that, at the price of further subjection, would bring us through all sorts of fantasies onto the starry paths.

We therefore dispersed on the eucalyptus and acacia trees of the slope so that each of us could observe a different starry region. At dawn we met to determine the causes of the movements of the heavens and to find the presumed traces of our father and the thanatobird. According to Atman, the sequence of galactic events changed very little except for the quantity of numbers and the degrees of the firmament's inclination.

Nergal and I covered the area between Andromeda and the Magellanic Clouds, where decrepit nuclei disintegrated into mounds of ash. Farther on there was Lucrezio who, little used to those signs, remained with his eyes half-shut to hear the meadow daisies closing in the dark.

Beneath us, clear nights opened on the grassy crags. Bethsam, in search of amusement, called out to us,

"Hey! Hey! Zephir! Lucrezio! Hey!"

He was sitting on an old eucalyptus whose top absorbed stellar smoke. Nergal, as usual, thought of mixtures of comets and flaming hearts of galaxies, hearing small branches growing around him, and blood lymph circulating in the nebulae and in the gaseous nodes. When Mansur lifted his eyes to the Cepheids' bluish whirlwinds, he perceived ciphers, hieroglyphs and logogryphs in them. But, practically speaking, he had abandoned us. He preferred to remain alone in the deserted little streets to await the birth of dawn amid the last bats. I believe he slept in the stables, on the hay, near the mules.

Nothing for sure could be found to explain our serenity, not even the red arms of the nebulae.

Orlando, relying on his strength, thought he could break the ties of gravity and detach pieces of gigantic Arcturus to project into the boiling galactic wheels.

"What are you trying to do?" asked Rowley, laughing.

Bethsam and Lucrezio amused themselves by bending the branches of the trees on which they were sitting in order to obtain an inversion of paths where hydrogen and helium condensed into sudden auroras and extremely hot rebounding jets. I too, in that position, had fun following the swellings of orange-colored Zeta Canori.

But the ascending and descending slopes were false yellow and white rivers. That is why Orlando, Lucrezio and Bethsam, struck by a mass of starry threads, fell asleep on the forks of the trees. Peasant ladies who looked up at daybreak and mistook us for saplings and foliage wondered:

"Is that tree still putting forth blossoms?"

We all fell asleep on the cherry trees and on the acacias. We were immersed in the blossoms that, because of their maturity, fell on the slope in crazy circular patterns when we touched them. I believe that our sleepiness derived more than anything from the intensity of the scents that increased at night and reached us even from the valley. These soft, lazy effluvia distracted us insensibly from the quasars.

Moreover, the most curious phenomenon, exploited by my sister, Welly (whose whereabouts were still unknown to us), was provided by the radio waves that struck the valleys, woods and rivers, making horned owls and lamenting eagle owls keep silent on the solitary crags. The lands of Qalat-Minaw upon which those sidereal signals bounced appeared more gloomy to us. This confounded the humor of the animals, the plants and the peasants who, from their hiding places, looked in astonishment at Aries, Capricorn and the North Star.

Since there was a rumor that we were always responsible for the stellar disorder, the peasants assailed us with the sound of clocks and bells in the towers. They began that suddenly and unexpectedly. At first, we did not find those alternating sounds unpleasant. They had various tones and, together with the rustling of distant nebulae, they spread about on the natural reserves of mountain water, in the deep valleys and in the maze of tiny paths.

"Ha, ha," laughed Orlando. "Who can be better off than us, far from everyone?"

Each noise was notably louder than the preceding one. Unfortunately, because of the lighter air and the mood of the peasants, after it grew dark the bells emitted gloomy echoes that made us bow our heads and rest them on the branches.

"Hey!" uttered Yahin. "Are you going to fall asleep?"

Then the sounds propagated in progressively larger circles and, over a long stretch, crinkled the leaves, which gradually broke off and fell to the ground. Since the above-mentioned vibrations could not travel beyond our mountains, the other territories remained silent. And so the bells and clocks of the churches rang throughout the vast expanse from the nearby towns of Scordia, Militello, Vizzini, Grammichele and, farther down, from Palica, and beyond that, from the south and north, from Piazzarmerina, Enna, Mazzarino, Càtana, Misterbianco and Motta. In an instant, millions of vibrations were absorbed by the trees, rocks, huts, torrents, and to these, in the night, were mixed the swashings of the worlds. When the wind was unfavorable, the sounds traveled with difficulty, with the result that young shoots crinkled more than usual.

Rowley laughed, with his pipe pointing upward, as he examined the variable velocity of the sound waves that seemed more merry and supple at dawn, more abrupt and harmonious during the day, until, as already mentioned, they languished at dusk on the offshoots of the west. To avoid being stunned by that perennial vibrating air, Bethsam, an expert in birds and their songs, and Rowley marked on tree trunks the scale of the times needed for the diffusion of the sounds.

Two days later, seeing that they were ringing the bells impertinently on the mountains and slopes of the island, and that we could not discern anything in the navel of the sky, dazed and sleepy, we saw some light mist rising from the western flanks. It grew thicker in the valley passes, and then on the ridges of the hills.

Some women said that to free us from those excessively loud noises, Aunt Agrippa had had recourse to her shrewdness with Al-Hakim's help. The bells imperceptibly stopped tolling, so that an indistinct echo lingered on the rocks and on the fires that the shepherds lit on the heights. Meanwhile, the mist increased, becoming granular fog that settled in the gullies of the lands.

So, there was silence. Assisted by my brother, Salvat, and by Pino and Orlando, Rowley, skilled in woodwork and painting, tried to make the planetary voyage pleasant for us. He therefore drew a rough sketch of the universe, painting with large brushes on the gravel, on the rocks and, without stopping, on the ruins of the Castle, on the low pellitory and on the eucalyptus and cherry trees. He painted, in the following order:

1) spiral galaxies in a vortex of flaming gold arms, or some that were bright blue with interstellar clouds that Orlando represented with countless purple lines;

2) elliptical galaxies, with violet embryos at their centers, flattened into disks of dead stars in which they revolved in search of a remote lifeless past; and Lucrezio, with one of his rough estimations, observed that in them one could sleep peacefully amid small plants with bilobed leaves, surrounded by the breath of foxes, centaurs and lions;

3) irregular nebulae, hot forges of stars, which Rowley painted very red among pebbles and pellitory, and blue-white on the crests of the ravine, where blooming capers proliferated.

Orlando, making Rowley burst his sides with laughter, spoke of male stars and female stars, the former solitary and locked in haughty circles of smoking plumes, the latter more talkative, at times sonorous like trumpets, and adorned in green, orange and white locks; and some with very long tails of noxious gases that quickly consumed and brought death to the nearby stars.

To stay within those natural confines essentially meant nothing. It was like sailing among islands and continents where darkness spread to unthinkable shores.

That is why Atman, after a day of reflection, came to tell us that it was useless to toil with those oceans of stars. If we hoped to find our father, it was necessary to seize the only law, the one law that regulates the beginning and the end of the magnetic bands and hurricane of atoms that form water, earth and fire. Being perplexed, we would have left everything in the hands of destiny if Rowley, Pino and Al-Hakim, the latter serenely sniffing tobacco, had not encouraged us to pursue what is within us and what is in the air and in the courses of subterranean swamps. But Orlando observed,

"By Jove, let's take a little rest."

And I:

"Orlando is right."

We wandered about the countryside. Often we lay among the clods with our heads resting on the couch grass and on the catnip tufts near the valley of Ballarò, whitened by mounds of chalk and old pine trees with sparse treetops. The scarp was full of hornets extracting nectar from the flowers of a prickly pear. Then they flew through the spikes and, buzzing, settled on the poppies.

We ate as we made our way, and Yahin encouraged us:

"Why follow tortuous paths? Let's harvest the grain. It's full of flour."

Late that day we returned to town. Sheep, followed by lambs, were grazing on the grassy slopes, and the women, seeing us, covered themselves. On the slopes of Qalat-Minaw, gusts of wind carried the fragrance of the grasses. Small lamps affixed to old poles gloomily lit up the street corners. Strangely, a pig at Itria followed us.

"Ha, ha," laughed Uncle Pino. "It's one of the few that have remained. It's full of sausage. Don't you smell the aroma of roast?"

We had fun calling that pig with childish words that everyone remembered his own way.

Orlando: "*Pdvplvl! Dagstn! Dagstn!*"

Bethsam: "*Filipik! Filipik!*"

Salvat: "*Pelinmic! Pelinmuc!*"

I: "*Fidreg! Fidrig! Mos! Mos!*"

Lucrezio: "*Rossossossosros!*"

And Rowley, with a nasal voice: "*Bedin! Belchin! Bedinbelchin! Savn!*"

It was great fun, believe me. That fat animal, without understanding anything, looked at us with small, carefree eyes.

And so we saw Qalat-Minaw like it once was, in our distant memory of a small town lost on a mountain and suspended amid the valleys. We stopped near a rocky slope where the night invited us to rest.

Looking down, I noticed that the fields were broadening in a large circle in which Sicily, Africa, America, hugging the equator, were forced to follow the solar declination. And I felt the earth spinning in its orbit with a sleepy sound that came from the lowlands, from the coasts, from the south and from the north, like an obvious trick of the mind.

XXI

Here is what we found out about Welly: With Geber, Canopo and the very lovely Mnemosine, she had suddenly left the deep valley of the Wadi Hamm and, reluctantly followed by our mother, Meliodor, reached Totosimic's squad.   Together, they all passed through the bleak areas of Castelluccio, whose paths were scarcely usable since they were overgrown with oregano that impregnated the hot air.   They went toward the grassless slopes, crossing the Ramacca heath, where, except in some patches of broad beans, it was difficult to find an inch of shade at noon.   Having left behind the few eucalyptus trees of the hills, the plain of Càtana and the moors with their clumps of ferns, they found themselves on the flanks of Etna, amid dense gardens that in the bright sun reminded them of their lost days.   The weak southern winds from the Ionian Sea below grazed the surface of the lands as they headed toward mountainous areas, where there are neither coppices nor marshes nor unhealthful exhalations.

Because of the great heat, windflowers were dying on the rocks, and orange trees burst into buds that speckled the fronds snow-white.

The soporific scents made little Mnemosine fall asleep.

Totosimic, as we had already imagined, decided to leave the area, not believing that tassels of leaves, sweet-smelling hyacinth and stellar orbits could help us find the *unicum* we were seeking.   I do not believe that our mother, Meliodor, feared a journey to the heart of the earth, having at her side her daughter, Welly, and Mnemosine, whose body absorbed fragrances and lights.   Geber encouraged the hesitant to continue the journey still farther up into Etna's impervious ravines, which were feathered with pappi carried up by the winds from below.   At night they left the chestnut and pine trees to advance into the solitary mountain. In the early hours the scent of distant fruits and the sea was sweeter than usual.

Gradually the landscape grew more arid, with lava flows and very tall broom plants with large yellow flowers over which the constellations passed.

When they decided to descend into the domains of the earth, the tides, from Columbia to Malaysia and from Japan to Greenland, leveled off, hugging the equator. There was no sun since it had passed from its zenith to its nadir, and in the evening the ebb and flow of the oceans redoubled along the circumterrestrial wall. Totosimic waited for the waters to recede with a retrograde motion, and we were already near the sixth lunar hour when the rivers returned with greater volume to the estuaries, increasingly filling the oceans and lessening their differences in depth.

"Now's the time," said Totosimic, as he looked from a summit at the coasts of Sicily, which were dark in the marine detumescence.

There were some who had doubts about the outcome, and among these was the son of Signa Mena. A few others were worried, thinking that near the bottom of the earth their sense of direction would be faulty.

Around them, foxes, ferrets and hedgehogs sniffed the ground upon which broom plants dripped their viscous humors.

Totosimic was proud because no one had attempted such an adventure before, that is, a journey into an obscure world where matter is subject to rebirth and corruption. They turned around to look at the farthest corner of the sky, which appeared blue to them in that darkness. All around, the rocks were condensing. At first they glittered because of their encrusted shells and the topazes and rubies that crystallized with the whiteness of salts; but then they turned from brilliant to infernally dark and hard, absorbing heat and loose earth through their thinnest veins. Many in the group were hesitant. Luckily for them, our mother, Meliodor, and Mnemosine, absorbing terrestrial elements limitlessly, reverberated a faint light that from gorge to gorge made even those desolate regions tolerable.

Not having vantage points from which to measure their distance from the earth's surface, after a few days they forgot about the voice of dogs and the whistling of blackbirds on the heights of Qamut. Mother's presence made them less sensitive to past memories, and so they felt inclined to cross new areas where stones hardened into irregular arches. They happened to pass through petrified forests with shafts of flint and under branches fringed with black crystals. And when our globe turned its face to the sun, the magnesium and aluminum rocks, infiltrated slightly by the solar wind, appeared violet. Our mother, Meliodor, spoke of the marsh Acherusia, and everybody, despite their very sluggish thoughts, wanted to reach it.

I don't suppose that they were always in the same place, because they felt drawn toward the declining terrestrial center. With a boreal latitude of 28°, 33' above them, they spotted, on an invisible vault, the tails of comets and the star-spangled nucleus of Pisces. Exhalations from caverns and parallel crevices outlined the dark silhouettes of our companions, through whom faint glimmers of granite were refracted. The men were met by clouds of atoms that, falling from their places of origin, were changing into fluttering, slightly reddish fringes.

I don't believe it escaped Totosimic that even down there, where heat and very black rocks are generated, they were all still bound to the circumsolar belt of the planets.

Some shepherds, for example, said that the travelers had succeeded in communicating with them through the changing motions of indeterminate vibrations; but perhaps that was nothing more than the buzzing of bees and the flights of ladybugs that in the last glimmers of the day took refuge in small yarrow plants and in vetch.

Going from abyss to abyss into dry basaltic rocks that had slowly grown into metallic lattices and stone leaves, they thought they would find, through black gold and veins of iron, the hidden traces of our father which, once out of the circle of air, dispersed in the amethysts and porphyry.

I do not know how long they descended, following Totosimic, who intended to reach Nife, where metals are generated in greater quantity, changing into concentrated fires.

But our mother, Meliodor, spoke of the marsh Acherusia, where they could peacefully lie down far from moons, noisy mountain winds and belts of woods. Around there, the small patch of land produced trees that encircled the area.

However, they did not stop, because magnetic currents and hallucinations reflecting in the lakes of iron and nickel continually hampered them.

Their thoughts became more and more incoherent as they fallaciously awaited the promised plain, where in a lunar dawn they would be united to the tenuous shades of our father. The rocks became harder, growing into veins that turned into black waves interspersed with whirls of crystal. Thank goodness our mother, Meliodor, tripled everyone's images with the beating of her heart and the sparkle in her eyes, making these images tolerable to their now untroubled souls. Mnemosine absorbed whatever arose in their minds, like floral memories or fragrances; and at her side, Welly struck the rocks and asked even the hollows, where dark waters seethed, whether the man-father still thought, whether the man-father still became distressed.

At times, when nothing wavered about them except a musty, stuffy atmosphere, our mother sang sad or sweet dirges, which, way up above, lulled to sleep serpents, scorpions, roots, and seeds that had never sprouted.

Seisms, shifting rocks, castles and villages buried for thousands of years, and surfaces swollen with lifeless drops surrounded the wayfarers. And since the crystallization of stones, aluminum and their own bodies were a single reality that extended above and below, they followed Totosimic involuntarily. This situation must have lasted a long time because Al-Hakim told us that our deep green valleys, the birds and the winds make up one and the same entity along with the earth and the terrestrial core.

All you had to do, in fact, was press your ear to the trunks of trees to feel underground tremors coming from the coverings of the roots, and to capture the stream of atoms emerging from the profound abysses down below. And so Al-Hakim, accompanied by Lucrezio, who was also paying close attention to such cracklings as he sat atop the trees, reached this conclusion:

Petals, pistils and stems fell as never before, even though it was late spring. Removing fragrances from the air, they disintegrated into thin eddies in the very midst of the clods, obscuring the spikes of wheat, and farther ahead, the gardens in the plains. Everything appeared bare and withered. Sparrows became sad, as well as the zephyrs, which made rows of vines, barley, oats and broad beans droop to the ground.

Al-Hakim maintained that, according to what he heard, sad messages came from the caverns and the subterranean nickel-iron mountains because Totosimic had not found the immortal principles of our father but rather a monstrous growth of very hard stone and liquid fire that left him trapped in rocks whose lava flows covered his body.

He, our poor relative and friend, was trying to rise from his distressful situation, but it was impossible for him to do so since he had become a mineral being without light. And he hopelessly watched all the forces of our earth which at one hundred thousand lengths followed the sun, duplicated it, mirrored it, playing a weeping harp.

Atman, Orlando, Salvat, Pino, Bethsam, Rowley and I looked at Al-Hakim, but he did not lose his composure.

Totosimic was trapped in solid rock, schists and slate. He was conscious and alert but certainly not unperturbed, given the fluxes of magnesium and silica that enveloped him below. Too late did he realize that the best condition for him was immobility, and that is why he abandoned himself in a hollow, resting his head and becoming continuously more petrified in a dense dark mass. He had become the image of himself. Nor could he summon his other companions, who could neither see nor hear, being attracted only by the indefinite trace that our mother left as she passed. And that earthen armor encrusted around him in a spiral that at first was muddy, then became dry as it hardened. The internal layers were made of chalcedony, while the successive waves were composed of tubercles and acidic slush. He called out to the others, telling them to change direction, dig him out and free him from that opaque material, but he was covered by a great number of blackish wrappings that besmeared even his hands, and spattered a veil of material in his eyes. And, all huddled up, he felt he was sinking in a shipwreck of memories within which he was rowing and turning into dense fire and into stone.

The others continued to move away, and never saw him again. I do not know how long it took them to emerge in the foregoing swamp, into which springs from the surrounding ridges sent their waters. These waters did not at all increase the level of the swamp's water, which, in its unstable mass, slowly moved in a timeless pallor. Asphodels were sprouting in small meadows in a vast area around there, creating a forest of white flowers. Following the example of our mother, Meliodor, the others sat on the bank, where they placed Mnemosine, who had fallen asleep.

Our mother sang, and the others imitated her, having neither shadow nor echo, and that was how the child, sleeping very peacefully, was swallowed up by the marsh Acherusia. Though she sank, she did not increase its volume but like an asphodel flower became dispersed within it.

They went on singing endlessly. Welly stretched forth her body and arms in the direction of the water. Mnemosine's body came and went with the slow waves, embroidering the surface with a cocoon of light and often appearing in the middle of it. Welly was saying:

"Can't you see?"

The child sank in the gloomy black course and then returned to the surface. The child's teeth were pearls, and her color made the group momentarily stop their singing. Our mother, Meliodor, said that they could not go any farther because there was nothing around them but waves and asphodels that were perpetually the same.

Welly kept stretching out her arms, but to no avail. Her little daughter, Mnemosine, was being consumed in light, rising and falling in that Tartarean sea; and, as she broke up into scales, nothing remained of her body but what looked like a shell gently transported by the current.

Everyone's attention was fixed on this as they stood motionless on the bank, and all they saw of that swirl was a white lump alternately appearing and disappearing. They remained there forever as our mother became a dry stone already polished by the waters. Everywhere the asphodels imperceptibly oozed black drops through their roots, leaves and tops.

Yahin felt moved by Al-Hakim's story. In fact, he said, "That's enough. What are you going around saying?"

The old farm manager Iaquino listened from a balcony overlooking the level ground of the Castle. Plucking fruits from an orange tree that grew from a mound and extended its crown over the roof, he asked,

"And then? What happened?"

Uncle Pino shouted at him,

"Quiet!"

Some chicks suddenly appeared before us, pecking at grass, insects and pollen. Then, heading in a single file toward the corners of the house, they cheeped, looking up at us:

"*Quidquid est in ovo est.*"

Uncle Pino, throwing a stone to shoo them away, cried out,

"You too?"

As the chicks ran, they looked at us with lively little eyes, and:

"*Quidquidest inovoest! Quidquidest inovoest!*"

To escape our boredom, Salvat and I stretched out on the ground. We were all seized by a feeling of discontent. On the scarp the mayflowers were withering, bending all to one side.

Resting my head on the ground, I smelled the scent of fallen pollen, snails covered with earth, turgid roots and tufts carried by the circulating wind.

"O Zephir," Uncle Pino called out to me. "Are you forgetting about your arthritis?"

I smiled. And it appeared to me that from the strata below fleeting voices and mute, ascending atoms were reaching me.

Naturally it only lasted a few seconds.

Having learned that, in Atman's opinion, we needed to resume our exploration of the sky to find the law of laws, Orlando grew angry and told us that he would leave us and no longer follow us in our pernicious errors.

"It's a muddle," he shouted, "a continuous running around that brings us nowhere. Out of a common mortal event, we've made a romance!"

According to him, it would have been enough to have a first-class funeral with a velvet-lined coffin, little orphan girls singing psalms and a band divided into two groups. One of the groups, placed in front of the coffin, could have been comprised of clarinets, violas, cellos, violas d'amore and string quartets that would play a slow and fairly joyful music. The other, behind it, could have been comprised of oboes and brass instruments, that is, a trumpet, a horn, a bassoon, a flute, a bass drum and a gong, and with a sad or very sad adagio played by a mournful piano. This would have created an atmosphere more suitable for coaxing the townsfolk to show up on their balconies and lean over the railings, and for making the first swallows pause on the rooftops.

Yahin, Bethsam, Pino and I listened to him. Orlando had gotten up. He said that the service could have continued up to the cemetery. As we have in part seen, that was a place which, after all, was restful and pleasant because of the cool shade of the cypresses, the fragrant petunias and the slight fog. He would choose that field as his permanent residence. And his dream would become a reality for the following reasons:

1) His wife would continue living on the mountain under which the valleys with their scores of passes gaped open, and she would thereby also avoid her *bellum perpetuum*. Since she would not be able to communicate with her well-named husband, Orlando, she would call herself "Suluk-Suluk," and finding herself alone at night, would take courage and raise her voice over the deep valley when it got dark, singing passionate love songs. In vain she would cry out, "Orlando, give

up your solitude and its rumble." With the new moon, the cliffs would become darker, almost pitch black, and she, tired of not being heard, would weave with her hands imaginary nests of wasps and spiders, and images of gazelles and onagers, of dead leaves, branches and blooming roses. She would invoke Ar-Rahmàn the Merciful, and to make him propitious, she would dimly light up the nearby valleys, casting in them handfuls of topazes, rubies and corals. The owls would gather around her. And in vain Suluk, drinking cinnamon and ginger tea, would cause the spring of Salsabìl to gush forth down there.

2) In so doing he could stay beside the remains of his brother, which were temporarily placed in Uncle Turi's tomb. And he would call him and speak to him in the evening when will-o'-the-wisps appeared from everywhere. And in a direct communication of souls he would restore his blood, which for fifty-six years circulated within him in the geometry of a system of canals; and he would again gaze at his brother Nanè through the marble slab, waiting for the moon to appear.

3) When some disciples of Asclepius or some literati died in the neighboring villages, he would collect their pneuma in the intestines of oxen, goats, pigs, songless birds, lizards and geckos that, swelling in these large and small membranous sacks for the propagation of the above-mentioned "spirit" amid the pale trees, could provide real pleasure for those who make life a *negotium* and not an *otium*. And he would invite the usual ten thousand priests and nine hundred and ninety-nine monks who, seated on the ground, on the tombs and on the cypress trees, and protecting their mouths with embossed shields to deaden the sounds, would sing abstruse psalms mixed with observations and reflections on the fleeting existence of things.

4) He could sit in the shade of those ephemeral trees and peacefully eat bread, black olives marinated in oil, and goat cheese.

Father Benedetto, an octogenarian, would use his white beard as a mirror to send him the light of the setting sun from the terrace of the monastery, so that the sunset would be prolonged there, reddening the tombs and the pastures on the slopes of Qalat-Minaw. Having finally achieved peace and quiet, he would persuade Muhallhel to put the finishing touches on that place with climbing roses, clumps of mint, small rabbits dancing in moonlit nights and small courses of water that he would turn into orange-colored streams on the left side, furnishing them with banks; and into green rivulets in the center, to bathe the emerging bodies of the chosen ones, to refresh them from their deathly turbidity and allow them to bloom freely as flowers that, unfortunately, would be sterile; and, toward the right, into canals of calm water, now emerald green, now violet, with beds of pebbles on which the stars would reflect their dazzling rays.

"What more could you ask for?" he shouted.

With a little boat, he would sail along those streamlets, stopping where the seeds of the dead sprouted better, to speak to this one or that and to tell them that their perpetuating themselves as ephemeral buds (naturally, on fake trees impregnated with the excessive humors of the bodies) was the best condition possible. They would thus escape the changes that things undergo, and become the substance of bitter berries, crystals and bark. And, more importantly, they could join the great rush of photons, hadrons and black and white atoms that came right up to those desolate terraces at night.

Orlando, setting out under the low branches of the linden in the clearing, left us. No one saw him again in town. Many said that he had settled down in that miserable embankment where bodies languished, the only good thing there being the air which traveled over hundreds of miles, coming from orange groves, wormwood plants, dragonflies sleeping in the canebrakes of torrents and from the billowy Ionian Sea.

XXII

Only a few of us were left. We wanted to quickly leave the galaxies with their radiant globes, nebulae and winged demons into which Atman was still tenaciously transporting us.

"Come on!" Atman said, as he pursued the stellar circuits.

Pino, Bethsam and I felt like we were entangled in a large spider web, and that we were no longer ourselves but rather expanding matter in murky matter. When would it all end, since everything around us seemed to be telling us that only the gods and Atman did not have an umbilical cord?

"What are we?" wondered Rowley, who preferred to remain on the lowest branches of a beech tree. The nights became monstrous. The summer dried up the few mountain springs.

"Come on, let's get out of here," advised Nergal, pointing to the trees. "What can we hope to find?"

Dragged along in that race, we felt transformed into particles and opaque vapors. Time and space had fused into a tangle of very fine electromagnetic radiations.

"What sort of bird can we hope to find up here?" cried Bethsam. "Let's get down."

At times he fired his shotgun to free himself a bit from the nightmare. At the sound of his shots, reechoed by the slopes of Qalat-Minaw, we heard the rapid whirring of some birds.

Hydra, Taurus, flashes of dying stars and smoky cauldrons—we had nothing else around us.

"When will we arrive?" asked Pino.

We had traveled over countless paths, going through airy valleys, through massive starry ridges, through infinite suns and infinite lights, and already below us we gradually saw the oceans of stars grow dim and disperse.

That wave of rivers which flowed into other wider rivers slowed down, and that extremely high flood descended toward the open sea which we had already navigated. We could not take in its circumference. Yahin shouted, "Let me return to my fields."

We had not been able to discover anything definite regarding the remains of our father and the thanatobird. I wanted to find the vital drop that had joyfully sustained me in past years.

We had reached the invisible limit of the cosmos, where past events coalesced in a time that was no longer time. We felt buried in wells of electrons.

Bethsam tiredly said,

"Let's sleep."

Pino:

"Let's sleep."

And my brother, Salvat:

"Let's sleep."

Beneath us the sky stagnated in a gloomy immobility beyond everything, and those oceans rose up with white horses that brought their shining manes into the other oceans.

"We are outcasts," said Nergal.

That must have been true, because Atman, who had always encouraged us, left us when dawn caught us exhausted on the trees, and some of us asleep on a large fork of a tree. More pensive than usual, he, followed by Rowley, left us. We went aimlessly from path to path, slithering under plants and biting their small branches close to the ground.

Since we were tired, Pino, Bethsam, Salvat, Nergal, Lucrezio, Yahin and I fell asleep on the cherry and plane trees. On the steep terraces the ripe wheat appeared red from the many poppies. Swallows, after having flapped their wings two or three times, let themselves be swept up to the three bell towers of Qalat-Minaw, and then down toward the sand of the torrents.

About sunset of the same day, while we, troubled, were looking at one another, we heard some whistles that made us turn toward the cliff. Emanuele, Muslim, Ziritia, Mariela and Gheorghy, who had been hiding under some boughs, arrived. Seeing that they had been discovered, Muslim said to us,

"What are you doing? Are you always up there? Why don't you travel around the world like us?"

Pino and my brother Salvat smiled. And the children, removing the boughs from their heads, came toward us to offer us some cherries. Rowley caressed Muslim, who was darker than usual because he had stayed so much in the sun. He asked,

"Where are you headed?"

"Ha, ha," laughed Gheorghy. "Up above."

A wind that carried the smell of salt and deposited sand on the mountains had recently arisen. Ziritia said,

"Why don't you follow us? It's a great game."

Atman looked at the children with half-shut eyes. All five of them ran through the plain, saying to us,

"You're going to be rooted to that spot."

I do not believe that they got their strength from the wind and its briny exhalations, or from the impetuous whirlpools that rose beneath us in a muddy shoal, but perhaps from the ardor of the sun, which burns more intensely in our southern territories. Preceded by Muslim, who was carefully banking as he rose aloft, they danced and laughed, and gradually took off. Our thoughts seemed vain to us when the children, sticking out their tongues to jeer at us, turned the horizon upside down with the rotation of their red bodies. Rising, they said to one another:

"Are we a circle?"

"No."

"And what then? Images?"

"No."

"And what then? The scirocco, we too?"

"Color!"

"Color."

"Nothing else."

"And a bit of memory."

Still at a low altitude, they spoke among themselves of a kingdom where strawberries, figs, watermelons, swans flying under the moon, onions stuffed with little fish, yellow quinces, dates, palms, numbers reduced to golden filigree, coconut meat, headless men and dense, tightly-shut saffron, all formed a unit with day and night.

In the increasing darkness of dusk, they were visible in midair among withering grasses and the plumage of birds. Their circle expanded in a rush of flashing reflections, with olives and carobs receding toward us. From the mountains a wondrous tension came forth which made the hills seem farther away and expanded the trees into plumes of smoke.

Yahin watched open-mouthed. Pino rubbed his eyes. Bethsam tried to rid himself of those images.

The air was becoming anfractuous and crenalated above the illuminated summits.

Mariela, the youngest of them, remained impassive, "outside" and "inside" being one and the same for her: an inexhaustible sense of ellipses and hyperboles moved by a red tide.

"Let's move on," suggested Ziritia.

"That's right," said Emanuele. "It's useless to stay with those ninnies. What in the world do they want?"

He was enclosed in a hemisphere of the sun.

"Let's draw close to one another," said Gheorghy.

"Let's go farther," ordered Muslim.

The light, refracting on them, gave things a constant curvature. Muslim, as if seized by a magnetic force, very quickly overtook Gheorghy and Mariela. Ziritia said,

"What are we waiting for? Let's follow him?"

And, swaying like a fine, soft feather, she followed her companion.

Then Yahin told us that nature had been distorted, sullied by unclean spirits and put in the grips of events that have neither foundation nor sense.

Since Mariela had difficulty putting herself in the rotary motion of ascent, Muslim pulled her up by her hand and brought her above the others. They cut through the air, dissipating the vapors of the sunset and continually rising above us. Cutting through atmospheric dust and extremely resistant plumes of colors, and, below—that is, close to us—rocks, fruits, trees, they (from their simple, established state of immobility), were transformed into indefinite shapes.

By increasing the speed of their bodies, they swelled into a new shape. "Let's swim toward Azdrak," said Ziritia.

She was attempting a speedy flight toward those mountains, amusing herself by using her fingers to build a small habitation of golden smoke within which she tried to curl up.

"Yes," Gheorghy replied, staying close to her. Then, pursuing an uncertain curve not easy to follow, he galloped gently behind her. Their images, sometimes clear and sometimes vague, intermittently drew apart and met one another above the red sky that predominated over the rocks and the crowns of the olive trees. Twilight rotated on the sandy ridges and on the clay formations punctuated all around by huge mounds of clods.

"Oh, don't you smell the scent coming from the valley?" Ziritia shouted. She turned upside down to let herself be permeated better by the aromas.

"Turlulù, turlulà," said Emanuele as he rocked high above the area at the foot of the mountain.

Whenever they flew close to the ground, they cut through spider webs. Following an instinct, they were transported westward, where the color yellow stood out in a fragile colloidal slime. It was almost evening, and all we could hear them say to us was:

"What do you want?"

"Where are you going?"

"Follow us!"

"Beyond things!"

"What are you waiting for?"

And the echo:

"for, for, for!"

And further:

"There's the sun! sun! sun!"

Attracted by preordained forces, they flew serenely, and nothing troubled them. By then hardly visible, they followed the paths of solar irradiation, preceded by Ziritia, who advanced with jerking instability.

Ibn-al-Atir, who wandered about the fields collecting edible greens, told us the following day that he had seen an unidentifiable group of figures flying over the crags and heaths. They were certainly not cirrus clouds in formation, nor cranes, because they collected too much brilliance from the airy strata. A wind, bearer of brine from the marina, and sand from the distant deserts of Africa, arose just then with a huge mass which was barely perceptible, but as large as about six hundred horses scattered on stretches of tuff and on barren lands. Rendering it denser was a sudden eruption from Etna that proceeded to send forth, from thousands of rocky ramifications of a distant underground, cinders, lapilli and changing rhythms of boiling lava. They averted that initial storm caused by the ghibli, arching or sinking through the already turbulent and hotly ventilated air upon which the lights of streams, of windows of solitary habitations, and of crags of mica were reflected.

From his friends the shepherds, who never rest and who set foot only in the most impervious areas, Ibn-al-Atir learned that it was a matter of flying children; they accelerated their flapping to reach the seashores near the gulf of Peloro, where tamarisks and violet flowers grew. They needed goodwill and strength to tirelessly follow the sun, which, subject to its destiny, left our earth and was undoubtedly dragging them to higher and vaster gravitational fields.

They flew for a long time, sucking the vapor of a few small clouds that condensed into gray whirlwinds only to readily disappear in strange eddies. I believe that the fish of the coast they reached stopped to gaze at them, since the fishermen in that area netted great quantities of hake, sardines, anchovies and tiny planktonic animals.

"Blessed be this catch," they shouted. And with one eye they looked toward the west, spotting something unusual in a distorted effect of wandering fires. But unable to lift their gaze much over the airy terraces, they thought it best to concentrate on the catch, which became extremely abundant.

For a while, Ziritia and Muslim were attracted by the movements of the tide and the rising crescent moon. The towns, which were not yet struck by the Egyptian wind, shone in the hollows and on the heights with reverberations that, despite the late hour, multiplied in small rivers and on crags.

"Who can ask for more?" said Mariela. And her little braid dangled in the wind on account of her speedy flight, as she wove ornaments for herself with the final rays that made the fish and the waves turn purple.

Emanuele was caracoling like a seabird, reflecting the entire turbulence of the sun onto the shadows of the reefs, which resembled the evening. It was a splendid mass whose image grew larger on the surface of the waters. An old fisherman out at sea asked himself,

"Is that a large sea gull passing over my boat?"

Ibn-al-Atir told us that, at that point, he could not glean any reliable news because men passed from the land to the sea and from the sea to the land on account of the redoubling of the bright haze of the evening. It was the kingfishers and the kites with their flights at great heights that gave him some information about the children.

"What nonsense are you concocting now?" Yahin cut in. And Lucrezio said that one can get signs of the arcane from the birds, and of this he was convinced because, at night, he was able to distinguish between the sleep of a robin and that of a finch, just as he could the hatching of the eggs of the former feathered creature from that of the latter.

In brief, it seems that they followed the sun's light beyond the confines of the earth and, running into a gap hundreds of miles long, they felt carried away in a distortion of time toward the east, onto the very steep flanks of our earth. They traveled a great distance; indeed, they left behind the Egyptian winds and the great peaks of the mountains, and left our world, free to explore the paths of earthly gravitation. And once they severed the ties that bound them to gravity, and were attracted and repulsed by other currents, they continued their flight in the measureless immensity of the solar orbit, no longer seeing the darkness. In this new situation, they found themselves transformed into small vermilion planets that were pierced and penetrated by that star.

That same day the shepherds, who from the heights of Le Coste were exploring fissures of rock where short, soft grass good for grazing sheep and goats still grew, saw violet flowers momentarily rain down from the sky. The flowers covered the crests and the valley, sometimes with a sprinkling of fluffy petals, and sometimes falling at an angle, unchanged, at their feet. The goats browsed indifferently on those flowers. But the phenomenon spread to all the mountain and sea towns of Sicily, to the Eolian Islands and the Pelorian and Ionian seas. Thus the people saw their horizon obscured because of that midday shower of buds and stems that, when the waters receded, covered the shores entirely, turning the mimosas, bulrushes and junipers violet. Shells opened to absorb the tiniest particles. And sponges attached to the bottoms of the reefs closed, along with the jellyfish nearby. Yahin said that Lucrezio and Ibn-al-Atir unscrupulously concocted perfidious conspiracies against the wise men among whom he proudly counted himself. Therefore, one had to find another interpretation for those unknown violet flowers which, in ridiculous numbers, had fallen on the heights of Qalat-Minaw, on prickly pears whose fruit was ripening, on dusty eucalyptus trees and on cockerels asleep beside vine shoots. It was the African wind, the harbinger of a great storm, that had snatched tiny rotiform elements and blue-speckled flowers from the seaweed and, twisting them into corymbs, had carried them along, inundating our island. It would have been better, with the excuse of complying with the changed moods of Atman, who had brought ruin to the town, to go to lower-lying lands, like Nunziata (where our companion often went, followed by Rowley), to work hard with hoes, spades, sickles and pitchforks, and to save, from the imminent storm, at least the broad beans, the barley and the wheat of Grandfather Michele's farm.

XXIII

That area, situated about three kilometers from Qalat-Minaw, is hilly and yields a harvest of olives, almonds and wheat. On the right there rises a spring whose mouth faces north, thus providing cool water in the summer. Grandfather Michele's property lies on a gentle slope. It stretches down from the left, where the soil is fertile and rainwaters descending from as far away as the foregoing Mount Carratabbía are channeled in a ravine of loose earth whose sides are covered with horsetails. Here large clods and apple trees conceal the propitious presence of a stream that flows even in July and August, when it is sweltering hot.

Two kilometers before arriving there, one sees a steep path on the right that ascends, in less than three hundred paces, to Giummarra, where there are stretches of limestone whose surfaces are marked with fissures and veins running in all directions. These areas extend eastward in gullies where Rowley had established his permanent residence. In fact, we found him there busily studying the courses of those very small veins dotted with blue crystals. In the past it was there where the peasants went to quarry the stone they used for sculpting women's faces, eggs, shrubs and ornaments with which they covered the façades of their houses.

Rowley smiled when he saw us.

"How did you manage to find me?" he asked.

Ibn-al-Atir grinned shrewdly, and Pino asked,

"What are you doing?"

With astonishment we saw that fair-haired Rowley, still obsessed with starry unions and the idea of eventually finding traces of our father, was using this limestone surface, made uniformly crystalline by the rise in temperature, to look through its translucent bumps and easily see the rising and setting of stars whose magnified images moved along below him. He was minutely calculating their passage with the hours of the lunar day, having divided the time it took for our satellite to make its revolution, into twenty-four parts.

All he had to do was lie face downward on the flat gypsum areas and look toward the bottom of the valley, so to speak, to follow the alternating movements of stellar tides and to measure their length, width and size. What is more, he had fallen in love with the "Southern Cross," which was bright, beautiful and devoid of false crowns.

At this point it was more instinct that attracted him toward those deep starry valleys than their scientific implications. In them he saw what looked like joyous fires that he could count at will and to his complete satisfaction.

In the daytime he used dead branches and leafy boughs to conceal the pathway of the stars, as he called it. And he no longer came to visit us, lost as he was in the pursuit of those games which, I believe, he secretly transformed into an abundance of numbers, proceeding to his astral inventory with countless points on narrow strips of white rock and on the limestone elbows. He considered the deep western ravines to be more suitable for his investigations, and he followed the changing movements of the galaxies, which were sometimes dense, sometimes dispersed. And in his enthusiasm, he unconsciously stretched out his tongue toward those sidereal springs as if to drink their silvery waves. When he spoke to the stars, he thought he was communicating with our father.

He assigned roof and foundation to those domes, seeing that many stars proceeded toward the center of Giummarra (beneath him, naturally) in vertical positions and in very brilliant paths.

In the daytime he marked on tree trunks, the half-hours, the hours or the entire nights he had spent on this or that side of the slopes which, vacant at daybreak and at noon, displayed an increasing number of lights after sunset.

The mountains around Giummarra, actually few in number and on the whole rugged, contained small veins of gold and celestial flints that, dissolving in turgid paths of sap, emerged in the small blue-green veins of the skins of figs and almonds.

If for hundreds of years no peasant had colonized this district, the gold dust would have been incorporated in the stems, branches and leaves, turning the trees into compact structures of scintillating metals.

He amused himself in naming the worlds below, marking them from the path with brushes of different colors when their orbits brought them close to earth. So he had stars that were friends—the majority—which he named and called out to in a voice loud enough to be heard:

"Rhodope."

"Ianthe!"

"Hecate."

"Calypso!"

"Electra."

"Leucothoe."

"Leucippe!"

He decided not to follow us to Nunziata because, in his opinion, the unexpected bad weather still raging, though intermittently, deposited sulfureous smoke on his path, obscuring his vision and fermenting the eggs of serpents. His presence was therefore indispensable lest the whirlwind bury the stars.

We left him. For two days we stayed at Grandfather's farm, there in the lowland, where some skylarks lazily took to flight. Atman, distracted and absentminded, spoke less and less. He was sitting under a walnut tree, near the small torrent where the thick, misty water was less blue and was evaporating in the corners. It was Nergal who approached him, asking him if his resolve had weakened and if he had finally become convinced that he had taken a wrong path.

"Don't you think so?" he concluded.

Atman said, in a few words, that instead of our father's essence, we had all followed figments of our imagination and Erebus, black with galaxies, without ever finding a trace of the shining egg.

While he spoke, he crushed some horsetails with his foot, keeping his head bowed. In his opinion, it had nothing to do with equinoctial or solstitial crossings, rotary spins and short-lived buds, nor with our common perspective, which was as high as the cypresses, as wide as the mountains and as long as the perpendicular descent of rays from up above, nor with space-time that couples night and day, a very sweet eros and thousands of magnetic fluxes.

"What's he saying? Is he raving?" Yahin asked me.

Uncle Pino kept silent. Bethsam had rested his rifle against the trunk of a walnut tree. Nergal looked at a leaf against the light. Atman left, for a moment, and went along the bank of the stream, crumpling the tips of the horsetails as he proceeded. Then he hurried back.

He said that he wished to leave that world-shell to seek the image of our father elsewhere and in some other way, because by then they had developed into millions of seeds in the thanatodimension, a fundamental component of human existence. It was not enough to decorate the temples to feel united to a supreme world. Instead, one had to view death as another shore of being, a "hereafter" of radiant force hidden from us, a state into which everyone retreats and comes to an end in his flowing universe. In that way, finally, the thanatobird and our father would forever be united in the same image. Yahin asked me, again in a whisper,

"What's he saying? Why don't we save the wheat from the imminent storm?"

That day, the wind blew into the valley with tremendous force. It enveloped the ripe wheat, made the sparrow hawks high in the sky go crazy and, twisting through the fields, shook the trees violently, severing the highest branches with continuous gusts.

It carried white salt, circulating its minute grains in the air.

The walnut tree under which we found ourselves scarcely managed to shelter us. Atman then said that the above-mentioned dimension transcends us and makes us rush forth in the opposite direction to explore with other forces that might help us determine its meaning.

He spoke no more.

Nergal bit his lip, observing, with a soft voice which became ever sharper, that we were looking for an immaterial substance that in itself had no activity or passivity but only the tight spirals of madness.

"Why?" asked my brother Salvat. "After what I have seen and done," he continued, "it's time I choose my own path. I think it's the best one."

Strangely excited, he explained to us that at that point he did not count so much on the search for fluxes without a spatial center, as on the possibility of circumscribing the lost semblances of our father in the terrestrial sphere.

"What do you mean?" Uncle Pino asked him, a bit worried about the storm that had begun.

My brother said that he, followed by a crowd of farmers, shepherds and seamen, would leave us to sculpt with the proper tools the features of our father's face in the alpine rock of the entire southeastern face of Etna.

Yahin heaved a deep sigh, lifting his head high. Pino cried out, "You've gone mad."

Removing from his chest the stubble uprooted by the ghibli, Salvat told us that this was the only way we would be able to subject the world to the model of our father. He could already see his pensive eyes, round forehead and sweet smile sculpted from top to bottom in the mountain.

"Can't you already picture the image?" he asked.

Sculpted in high relief, as he imagined it, it would not weaken under gusts of wind, nor would its reality ever be extinguished from one generation to the other. Surrounded on all sides by Etna's wall, in the shadows and lights of the lava, and having protrusions and indentations, it would clearly stand out from the rocks.

That face would not be a quantity of things, nor would it generate things. It would be the One to which the peasants of the island, the birds, the trees, the fish in the sea could readily turn to contemplate themselves. Nor, then, would anyone experience fickle loves and the fatal caducity of life. The impenetrable mountain vegetation, hugging all around our father's image in a variety of colors, would make it blaze forth clearly with the setting sun.

During the night, the smells of the sea emanating from the waves, and the stars above, opposite the earth, would make swarms of gods emerge from our immobile father, and while still following the impulse of their common origin, would swirl through the shadowy things of the world.

According to Nergal, that sort of reasoning was uncalled for in that only with man-tree grafts could we elude chaos. We would thereby realize two goals. First of all, we would free the earth from people who, believing that they were pursuing love, peace and science, were unwittingly and exclusively striving to decompose matter through the well-known "mouth-anus" circuit.

Through the concerted effort of people's teeth, oxen, goats, horses, donkeys, cats, frogs and mice are pushed into the stomach, and from there, in the form of fat mush, to the liver, and then around the heart, expanding in the form of blood through veins and arteries. And one should not forget chicory, wheat, millet, water, salts, wine and rum, that mix in with the above-mentioned foods, filling and emptying the intestines, which act like ingenious machines. Pouring into the blood in the cardiac cavities in an inverse current from the heart to the auricles, and from there to the heart and lungs, they leave the anus as waste products after having dispelled a stream of common thoughts out of the left cerebral hemisphere and out of that of the right, allowing the fibers of which our body is composed:

to contract;

to dilate;

to sleep;

to bend into curves and oblique skeins of tendons and nerves.

Yahin again asked me in a whisper,

"Is he delirious too?"

Secondly, continued Nergal, we should reverse that cycle, not a difficult task, given what we accomplished with Aramea and her son. We could soften cartilage, render tendons flexible, reduce the tiring pulsation of the brain to the lowest common denominator, and from this grinding and ever-mobile machine we could obtain green joints and watery humors with the simple nourishment of terrestrial humus. On high we could encase men (without their bones) in the spongy pith of trees. Then we could riddle them with holes and stomas so as to achieve another reality, one which is bearable and different from the massive structure that perpetually follows the systoles and diastoles of blood and tissues, thus having the exact same fate as that of stellar universes.

Uncle Pino looked at Nergal askance. Atman paced back and forth in the shadow of the walnut tree, under the first gusts of sand. Bethsam said,

"Because of that unfindable bird, one can't understand anything anymore. I'll go around slaughtering birds. You can go around looking for them all you want, but you'll never see them again except in the graffiti I'll leave in ravines and on rocks.

Nergal tried to convince us. He said that something of the human skein would be left in the form of tapering elements lumped together in the sap, and in that of budding plumules, tall arboreal branches, twigs and scales. So why become discouraged? On the other hand, we would not have to put up with discharges of gas, violent amorous passions and grave emotions and actions. Instead, we would see new organisms festively exciting and perfuming the countryside with harmonious zephyrs, scarlet inflorescences and silvery human pupils that would make the stems and the tips of leaves sway. Yahin stretched out his arms toward the sky.

He added that we could alternate the bright color of an individual with his more somber color, in white buds, small roses and barkless knobs.

"What more could you want?" Nergal shouted at us.

His fervor weakened. He no longer knew what bizarre animalvegetal inventions to have recourse to. He understood that an island such as ours could not reduce itself to a jumble of limbs and branches, since for millions of years it had received impulses from the sea and the woods. So he pointed out that for the few chosen ones he had planned the creation of sensitive dwarf trees which, reaching the height of an inch, would delight us on account of their small downy branches and miniature fruit. He listed:

a festive apple tree, a few centimeters tall, with small whitish grains for apples;

a Japanese medlar that would adorn the sides of ditches;

a "seven-in-the-mouth" pear, half a meter tall, whose small globular fruit would gradually takes on color;

a yellow quince which would rise one foot from the ground;

a clementine, a blend of orange and tangerine, a few centimeters tall, and therefore so tiny that it would not be noticed were it not for its orange blossom scent;

a sweet early fig, as well as a pale green fig, a "snake" fig and a Valencia fig—all dwarfs and so small that they would bend if a lizard should pass by;

fir trees, with their myrrhs and balsams, that a few grams of snow would be enough to cover;

lacustrine poplars full of snails because of their shortness;

olive trees, soft and gray, that would be submerged by a gush of water because of their smallness;

almond trees that would blossom in the space of an hour;

Neapolitan medlars that would grow to the height on one foot, not more;

hawthorns that would be visible to the human eye only if gathered into many large bundles;

climbing rose trees that would be visible only to ladybugs and would be easily mistaken for the red elytra of the latter.

As Nergal began to speak of gluttonous bees, locusts and spiders, we heard an unusual flutter. Bethsam looked in the direction of the hill of Doniaià and said to us,

"Do you see that?"

Freeing itself from a whirlwind, an unknown stray bird, in a measured number of turns, soared in the great sea of clouds that had gradually accumulated on the hill.

"I'm going to shoot!" shouted Bethsam.

"He aimed his rifle, but Nergal, putting aside his countless fantasies, stopped him.

"What are you doing? Have you gone mad?"

"You shouldn't shoot at random," Uncle Pino said to him reproachingly.

Gazing silently at the sky, we all realized that it was an eagle cutting through the air from south to north and heading for our group. It was being ridden by Al-Hakim.

"Hey there," exclaimed Yahin.

The flight was calm, despite the bad weather, and the reflections that the eagle cast on the countryside gave us an innocent delight. The Arab was already waving at us. Meanwhile, the bird, flying both high and low (and thus avoiding the impetus of the gusts as much as possible), approached us, continually and intentionally grazing the sides of the thousand-year-old olive trees so as to make whirls of leaves fall. It landed in the middle of a wheat field.

Bethsam, in his astonishment, remained there with his rifle against his shoulder.

"What do you want, Al-Hakim?" asked Yahin. "Are you bringing us some good news?"

The Arab smiled and, pointing to Nergal, said,

"What are you waiting for? Everything is ready up there."

"Are you trying to discredit us?" yelled Pino.

Nergal, actually a bit annoyed, said that since he hadn't been able to convince us to create an immutable, carefree nature with multiple characteristics, he was forced, despite himself, to leave us forever. Waiting for him on the Ereian summits was Kid, his assistant, whom everyone knew; the white-haired poet, Amr-el-qays, who in the dunes of the desert intended, with his help, to create banks of dense white poplars and palms along the rivers, where he would sing of love and gardens like the good ruwat he was; the centenarian Gorgia, who would persuade him with his words, beguiling the mind, that nothing human exists if not suffering and whimsical ideas, so that it would be better to put aside fear and tears, and refresh ourselves with laughter among our dense trees; and finally, Al-Hakim himself, who, to free us from grave worries and incurable madness, would render the spirits of trees propitious to us.

After saying that, he mounted the eagle, which rose up in eccentric ellipses. And before we could no longer hear the sound of his voice, Al-Hakim informed us that on the Nebriode, Madonie, Peloritani and Erei, and even farther below in the foothills, the peasants and shepherds were waiting for them. These people, informed that that which is, is that which is not, were already searching the horizon to see them appear at the time when evening would bring the ascending node of the moon along with Aries, and to welcome them from the mountain passes and heights with bonfires and the music of very pleasant flageolets.

Uncle Pino exclaimed,

"Al-Hakim, you've destroyed everything. What can we now hope to find?"

The eagle had already made its first turns.

The Arab, putting his hands in front of his mouth like a funnel to make himself be heard, told us that even the vigilant owls, full of curiosity, would look at them from the bottom of their holes. They would fly still higher, over the minute dust that came from the African coasts and was that still arriving on the lands, and they would peacefully see it rise above us.

The bird, moving turbid air currents, left the wheat fields, rose above Grandfather Michele's olive grove and, after hovering a moment above the hill, began a rapid flight, going against those same winds.

During that day the winds increased and, striking the barren hill in front of us, blew in oblique gusts, rising over the very low thickets of sorghum.

We went back into Grandfather's house, in front of which there was a fig tree and some small plots full of bellflowers. The weather was pleasant even though the southwest wind gusted over the roof tiles, bringing over the countryside a great quantity of fiery dust and whorls of salt carried from the seashores over very great distances.

Ibn-al-Atir, having joined us, explained that the fierce cyclone was growing larger over the saltwater lakes and over the entire countryside of the island. The chicory picker, stringing little white and black stones which he intended to sell to the women, said that it was useless to get angry, because nobody can do anything to change destiny. After opening the window to show us the lands where the wind was growing stronger, Atman observed that it is not outside where one should look for the origins of sweet memories (and in this Nergal was deeply mistaken) but inside of us, in an inconceivable velocity and in infinite wells of immutable white eggs.

"Are you at it again?" exclaimed Yahin. "Don't you see the bad weather all around us endangering our few crops and plantations?"

Atman paid no attention to him. He added that, through our eyes, our muscle fibers and our brain, we filter thought waves that come from the outside in the form of tiny particles, buds, light and darkness, but all this is meaningless if one does not experience it with different states of mind. There, finally, everyone finds the remains and affluences of our father.

"You're trying to drive us completely mad," observed Uncle Pino. "I'm waiting for this storm to end so that I can travel again to the markets to sell oxen, lambs and colts as in the past.

It was not yet the ninth hour when Atman, unbeknownst to us, left us. The wind, blowing ceaselessly over large areas, brought reddish sand in midair that was greatly restrained by the maze of branches and leaves in the woods around Qalat-Minaw. Spinning, it revolved around the axis of Sicily and, hiding the southeasterly area of the Mediterranean, obscured the solar disk with a changing swirl of salt and sand. During that day, which slowly, very slowly waned, one could no longer discern the topography of the countryside, and even the deepest ravines were covered with dust. The few birds still visible were unable to withstand the force of the whirlwinds into which they were precipitously flung despite their attempts to flee.

Lucrezio told us that judging by the darkness surrounding us, and the reddish sky to the west, the storm must have struck not only Africa and Sicily but also oceans and extremely vast stretches to the south, north and east on which, ever more dispersed, the terrestrial lights became smaller. Furthermore, all you had to do was call out to someone for your voice to reecho from hollow to hollow in the thousands of gaps. It must have been the scirocco, the southwest and the austral wind unleashed together. The mountains and forests were unable to mitigate the storm. Indeed, in the lowlands and marshes one saw briny dust mixed with sand encrusting the trees and rocks.

We never found out how long Atman managed to walk through the ghibli, which inflamed and fermented the fodder, wheat and swamps. I can only tell you that no one heard of him again, nor did anyone ever find out in which direction he had headed, or whether a great quantity of sand had deposited itself around him.

After a few days the horizon became less cloudy and brighter because of light sea breezes, but if one walked through the heaths and gardens, as Ibn-al-Atir and Lucrezio did, one could still see the unhealthful air prevailing, which, after crossing the equator in its natural movement, spread from country to country until it reached the Arctic and Antarctic poles. Then, growing darker as the hours passed, it obscured the rising moon and the wandering constellations.

December 1968—April 1970

About the Author

Giuseppe Bonaviri was born in Mineo (Sicily) in 1924. His father, Settimo Emanuele (Don Nanè), was a tailor who wrote poetry, and his mother, Giuseppina nee Casaccio (Donna Papè) was a housewife whose extraordinary talent for recounting ancient tales fired the author's imagination at an early age.

After completing his elementary education in his hometown, Bonaviri attended a secondary school in Catania and then enrolled at the university there, receiving his degree in medicine in 1949. He worked as a physician in Mineo for seven years, specializing in cardiology, and served as an officer in the military at Casale Monferrato (Torino) for the next two years. He then settled in Frosinone, where he has been residing since 1957, dedicating himself both to his medical practice as well as to creative writing. He is married to Raffaella Osario, has two children (Pina and Emanuele) and one grandchild (Gianluigi).

Bonaviri began writing poetry when he was about eight years old. His literary debut took place in 1954 with the publication of the novel *Il sarto della stradalunga (The Tailor of Long Street)*. His numerous successive works in several genres demonstrate his unceasing dedication to literature: *La contrada degli ulivi (The Area of the Olive Trees)* (short stories, 1958); *Il fiume di pietra (The River of Stone)* (novel, 1964); *La divina foresta (The Divine Forest)* (novel, 1969); *Notti sull'altura (Nights on the Heights)* (novel, 1971); *Le armi d'oro (The Golden Arms)* (long short story; 1973); *L'isola amorosa (The Loving Island)* (novel, 1973); *La Beffària (Hoaxville)* (novel, 1975); *Follia (Madness)* (youthful play, 1976); *Martedina (Martedina)* (novel, 1976); *L'enorme tempo (The Enormous Time)* (novel, 1976); *Dolcissimo (Dolcissimo)* (novel, 1978); *Il treno blu (The Blue Train)* (short stories, 1978); *Il dire celeste (Heavenly Words)* (poems, 1979); *Nel silenzio della luna (In the Silence of the Moon)* (poems, 1979); *Novelle saracene (Saracen Tales)* (fables, 1980); *Di fumo cilestrino (Of Pale Blue Smoke)* (poems, 1982); *O corpo sospiroso (O Sighing body)* (poems, 1982); *Quark (Quark)* (poems, 1982); *L'Incominciamento (The Beginning)* (poems and tales, 1983); *L'arenario (Sandstone)* (essays, 1984); *L'Asprura (Aridity)* (poems, 1986); *E' un rosseggiar di peschi e d'albicocchi (The Blush of Peach and Apricot Trees)* (novel, 1986); *Il dormiveglia ('Twixt Sleep and Wakefulness)* (novel, 1988).

Besides publishing these volumes, Bonaviri also contributed scores of critical articles, reviews and narrative writings to newspapers and literary journals. Moreover, he has traveled extensively throughout eastern and western Europe, presenting his works and giving lectures. In 1987 he also visited the United States.

Among his prestigious honors is the Premio Selezione Campiello, which he received in 1978 for *Dolcissimo*. Recently he was also nominated for the Premio Strega, and for the past several years has been one of the leading Italian candidates for the Nobel Prize in Literature.